Sugar Skulls Shits
A Swear Word Adult Coloring Book

Adult Coloring Book J. Kaiwell
And
John Daniel

Published by PUBLISHING COMPANY in 2016
First edition: First printing
Illustrations and design © 2016 Adult Coloring Book J. Kaiwell

allcoloringbook.com

ISBN-13: 978-1533590039
ISBN-10: 1533590036

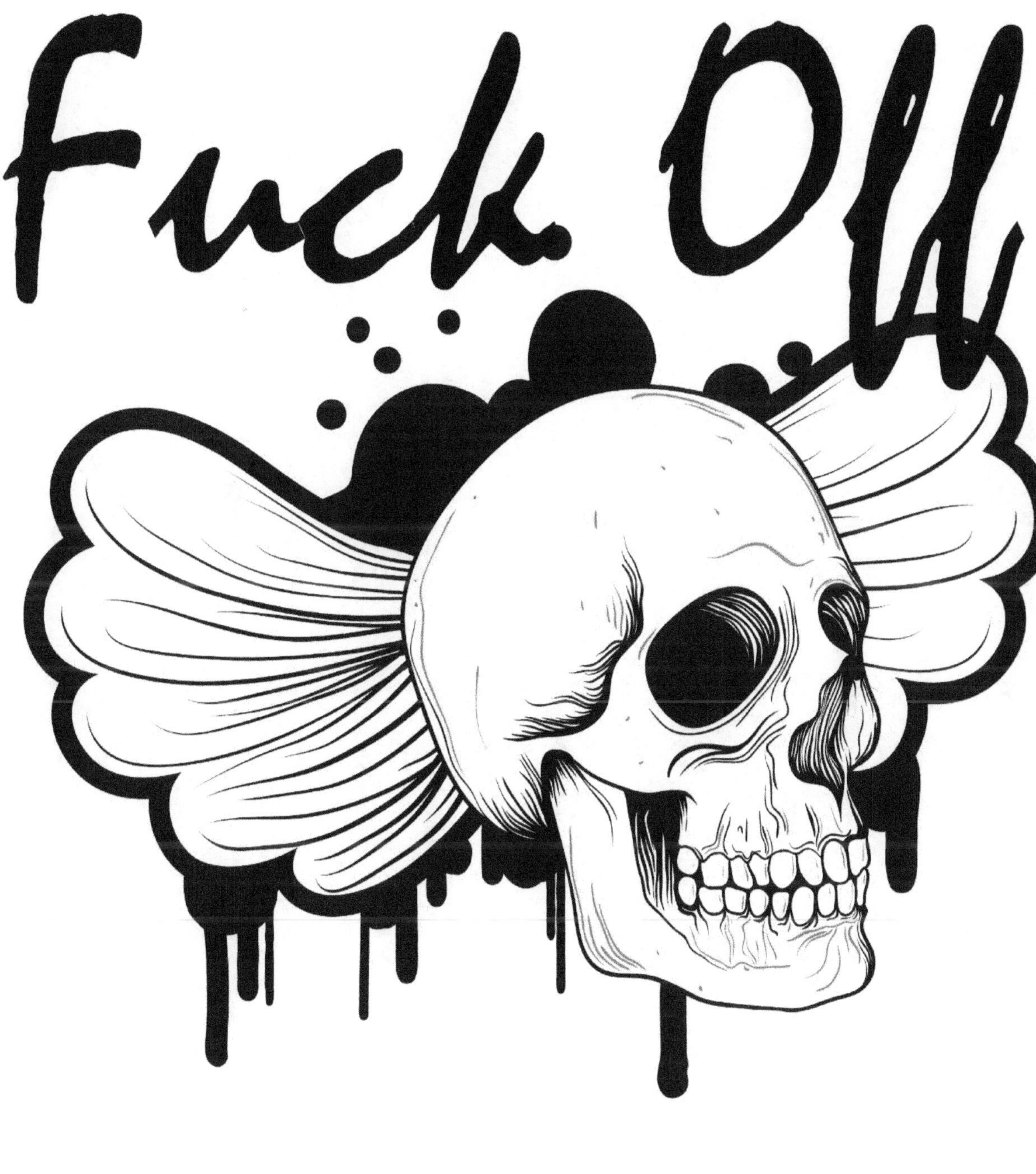
Fuck Off

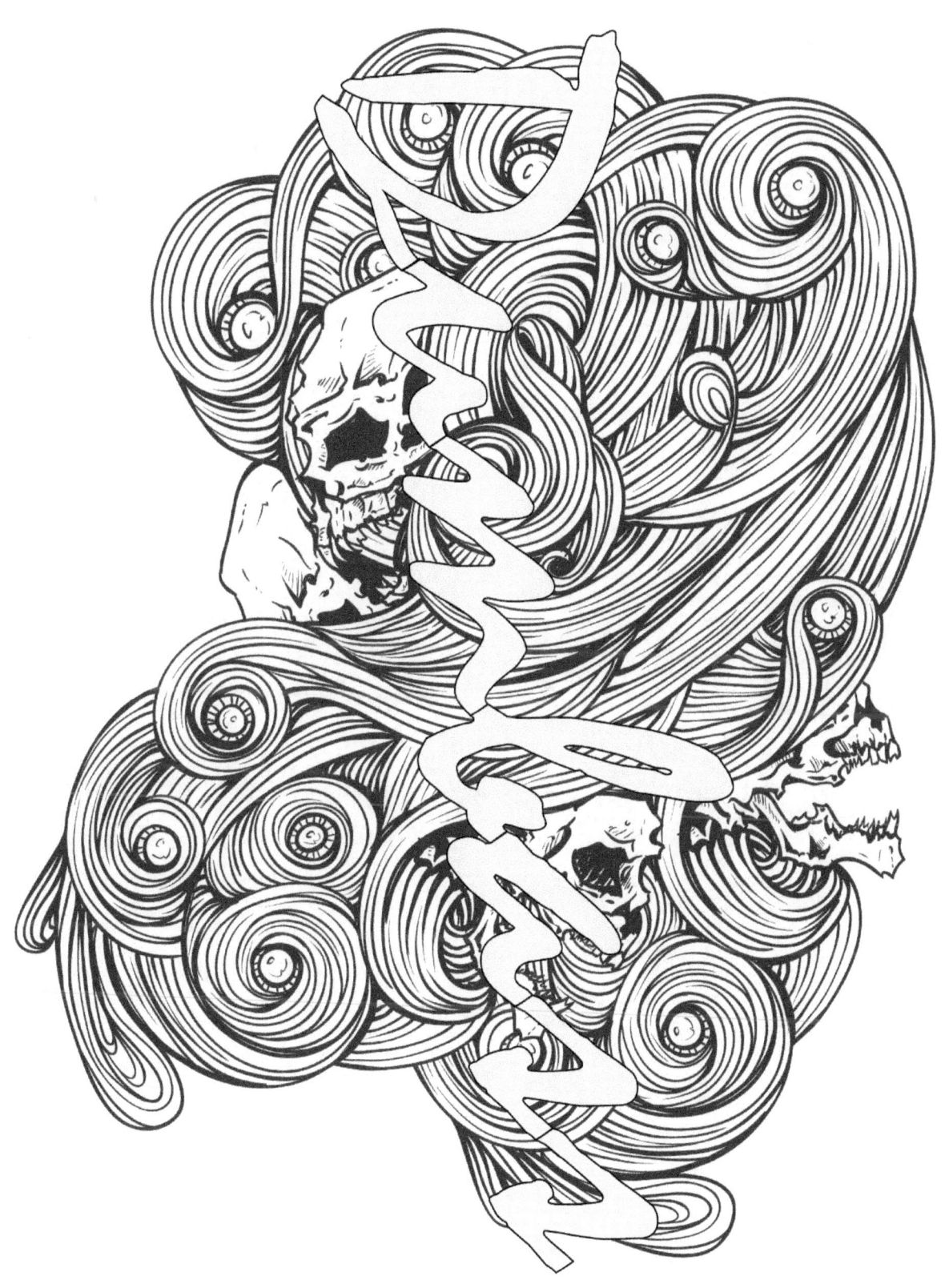

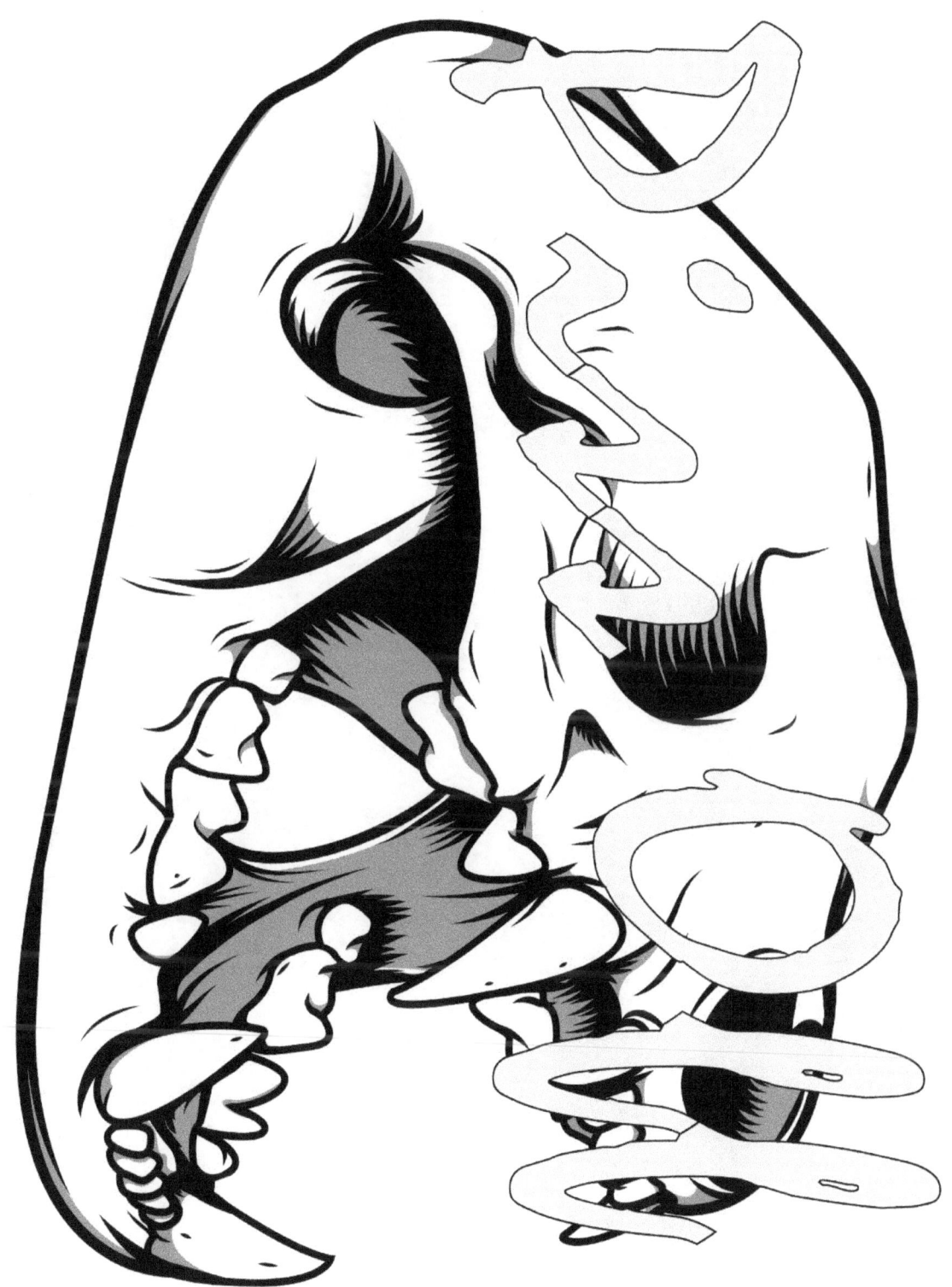

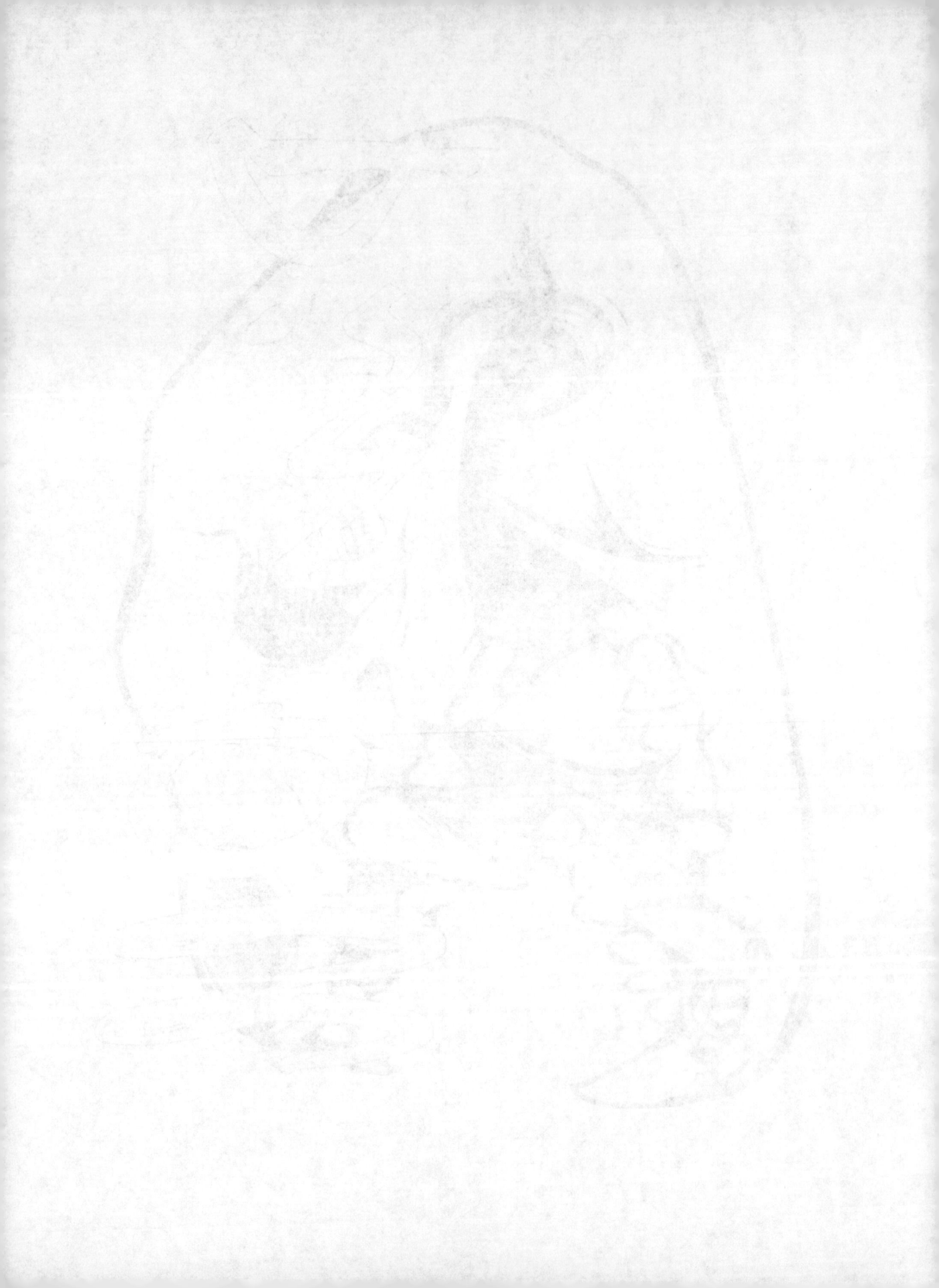

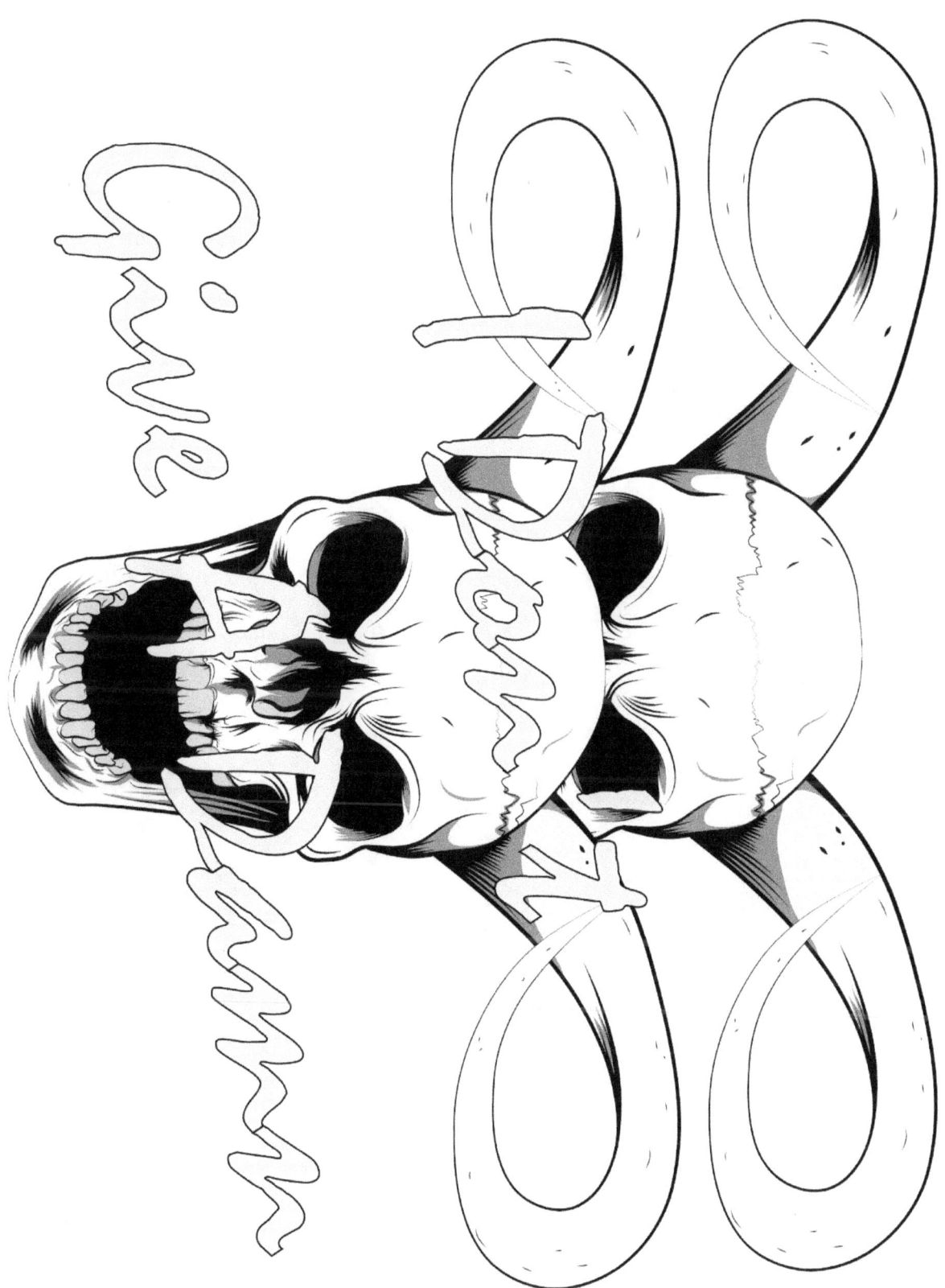

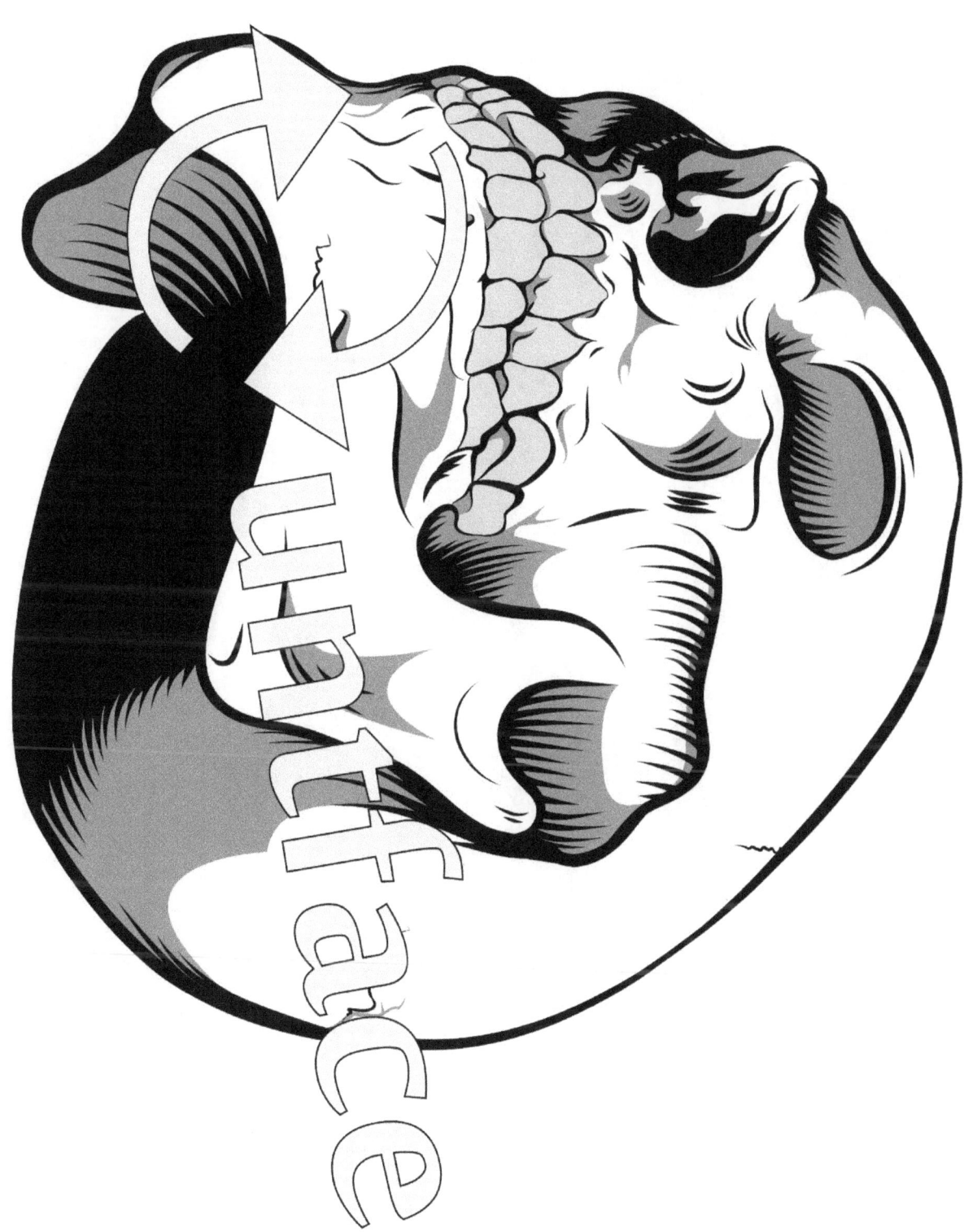

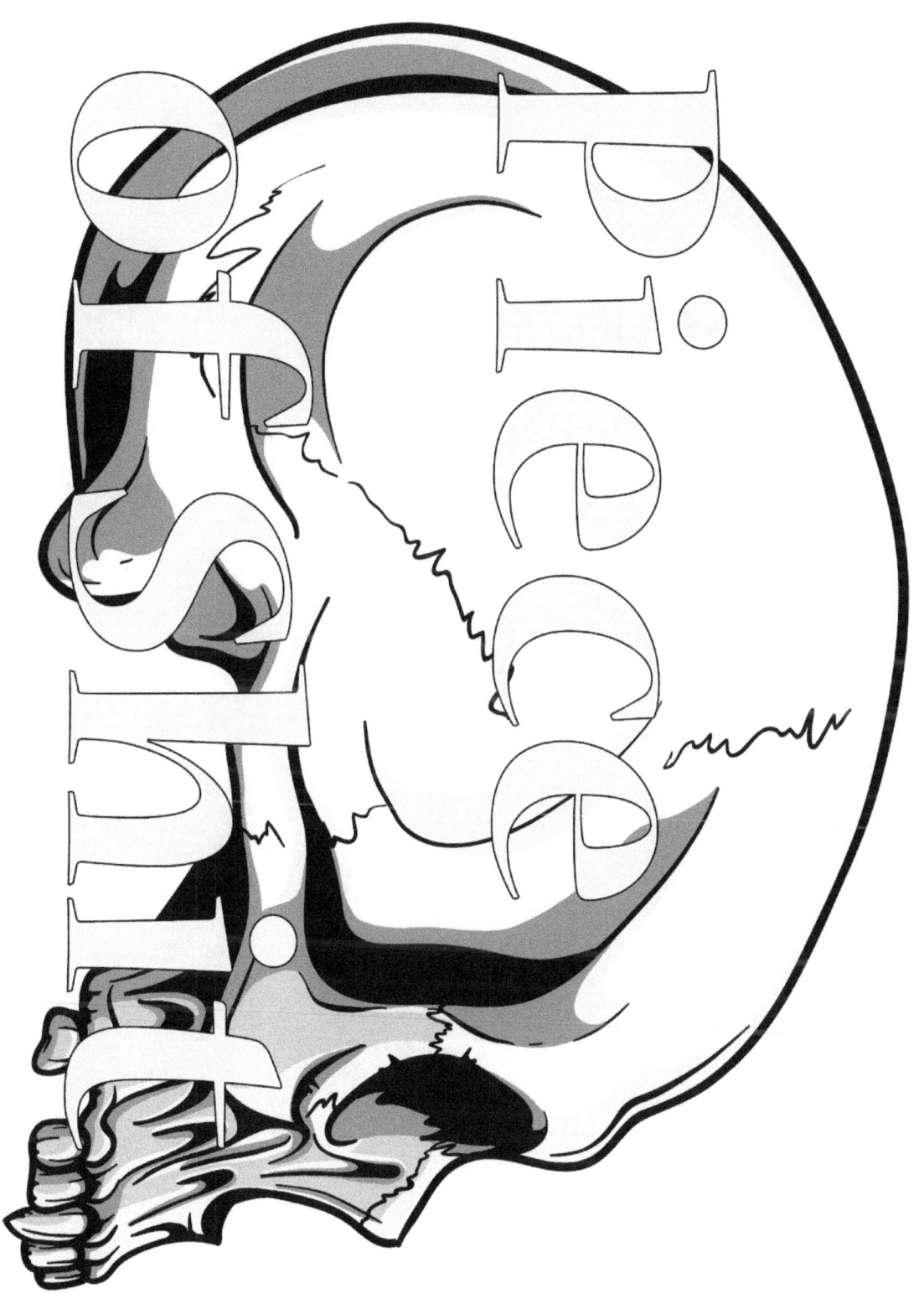

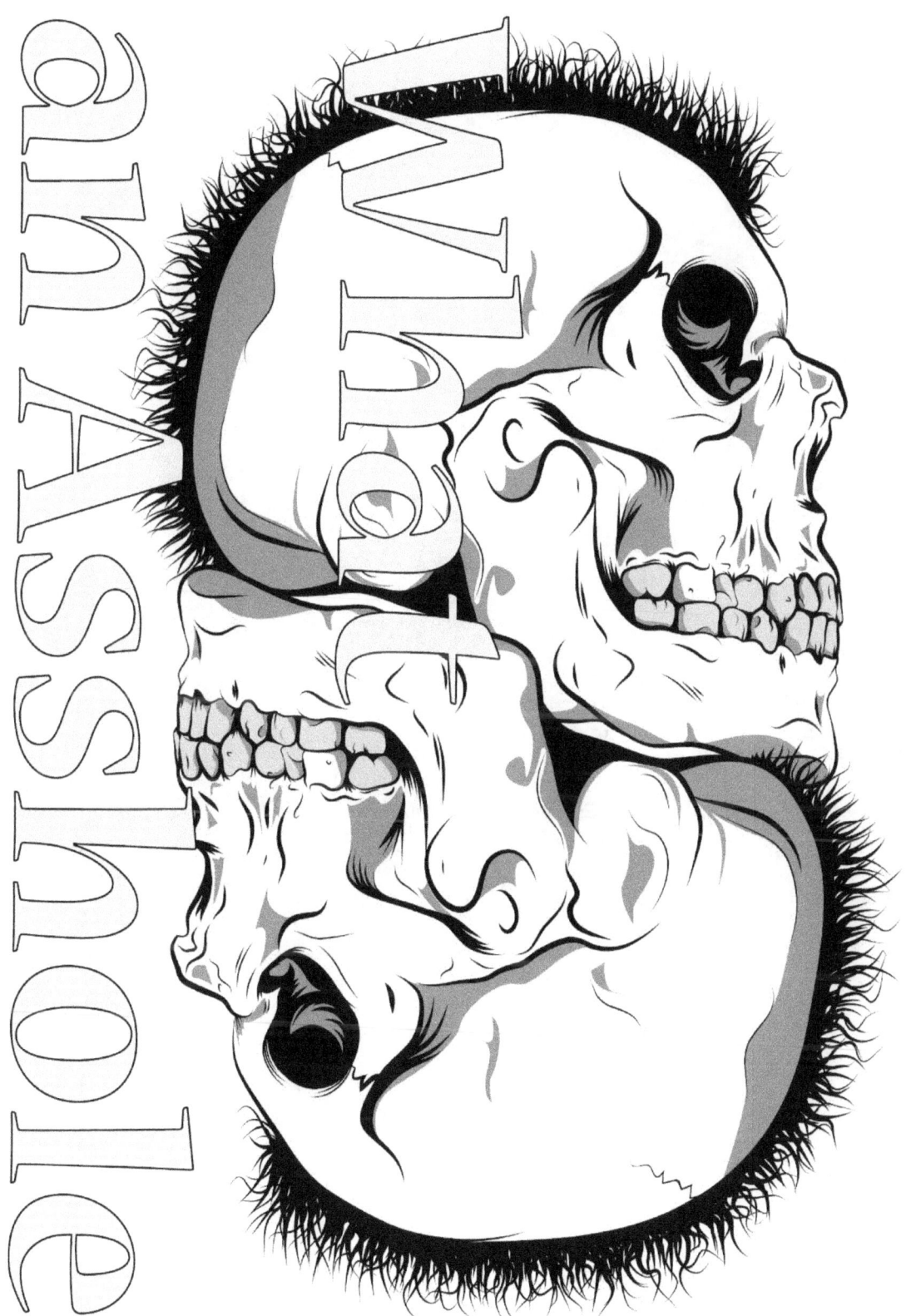

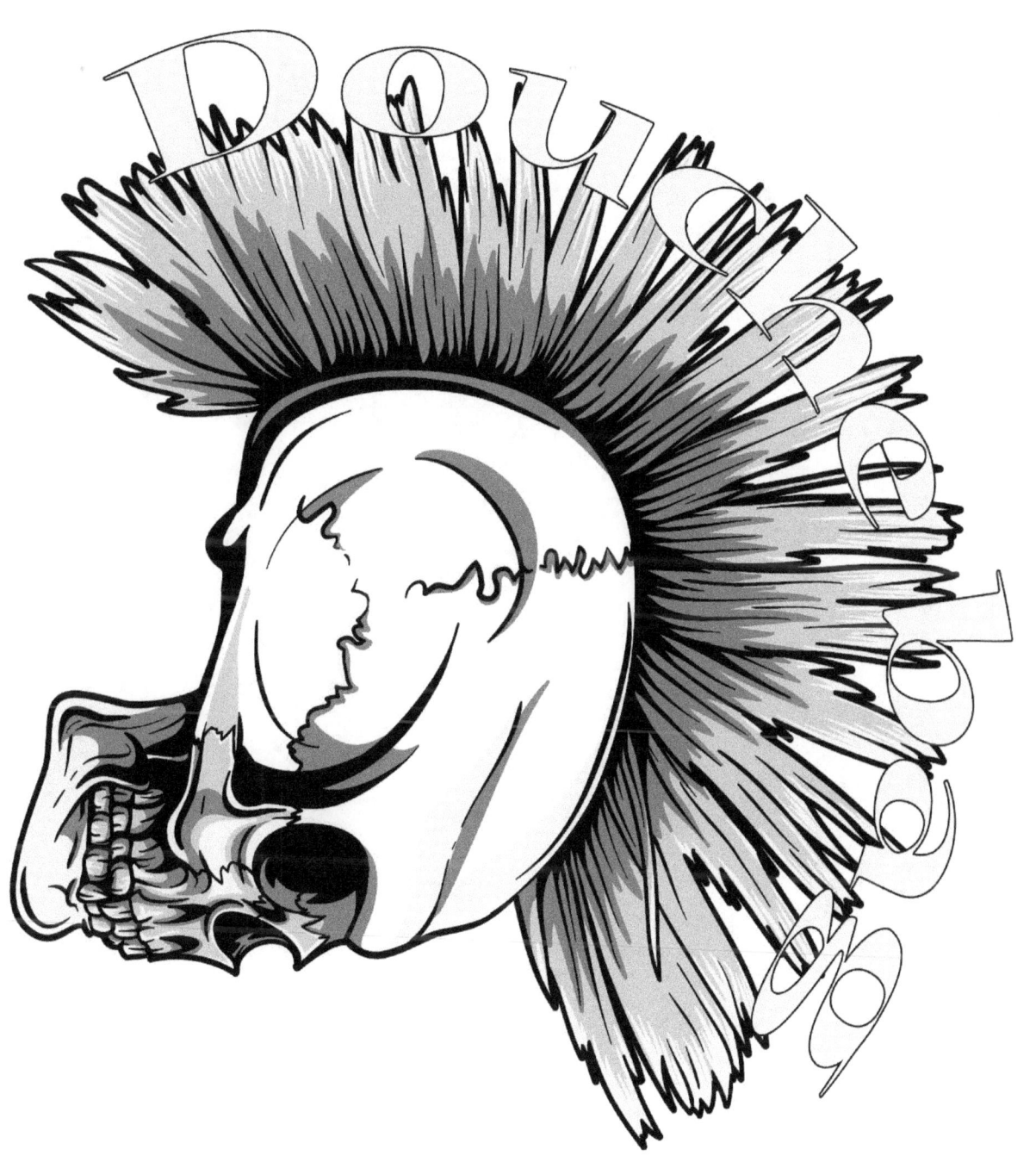

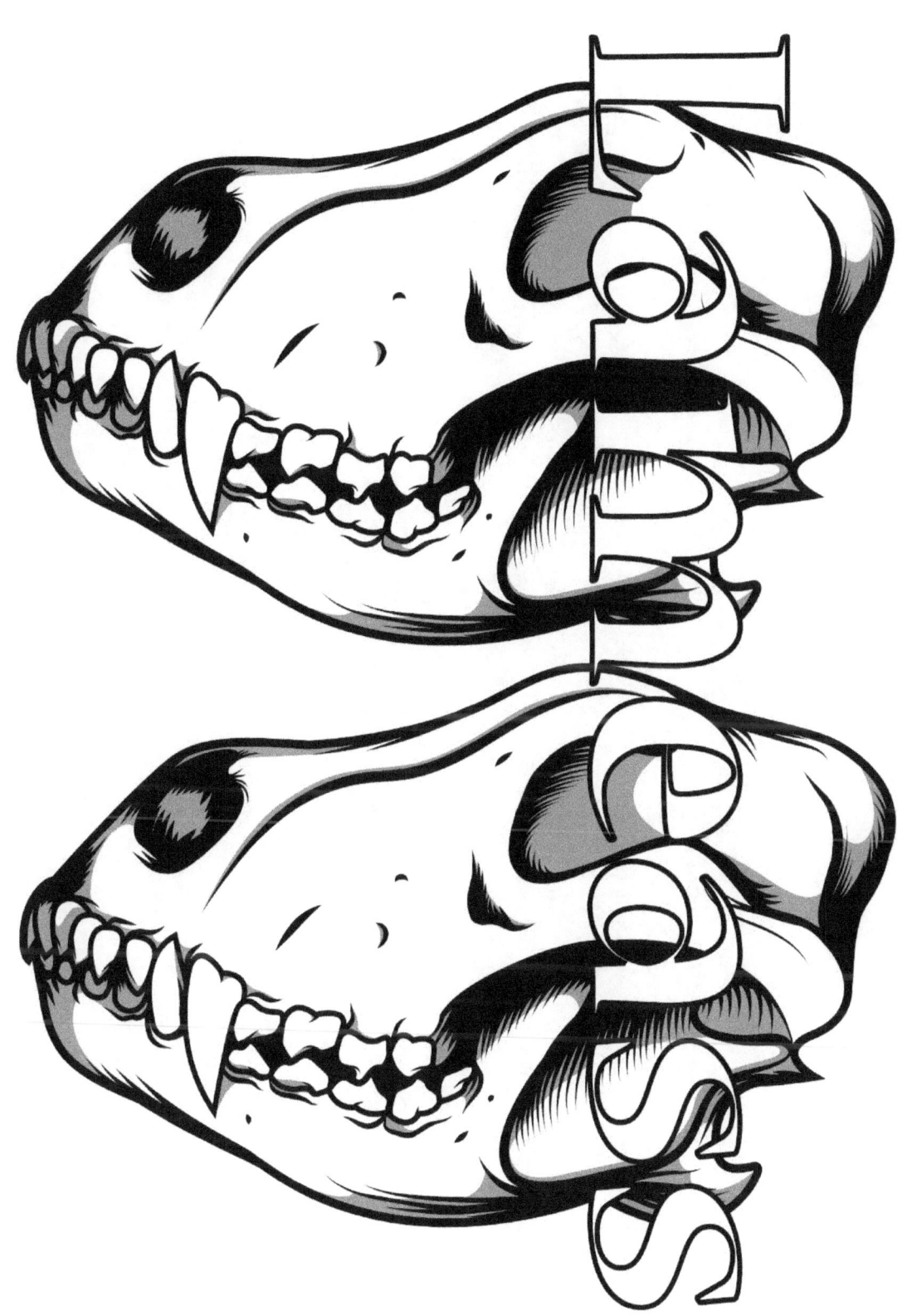

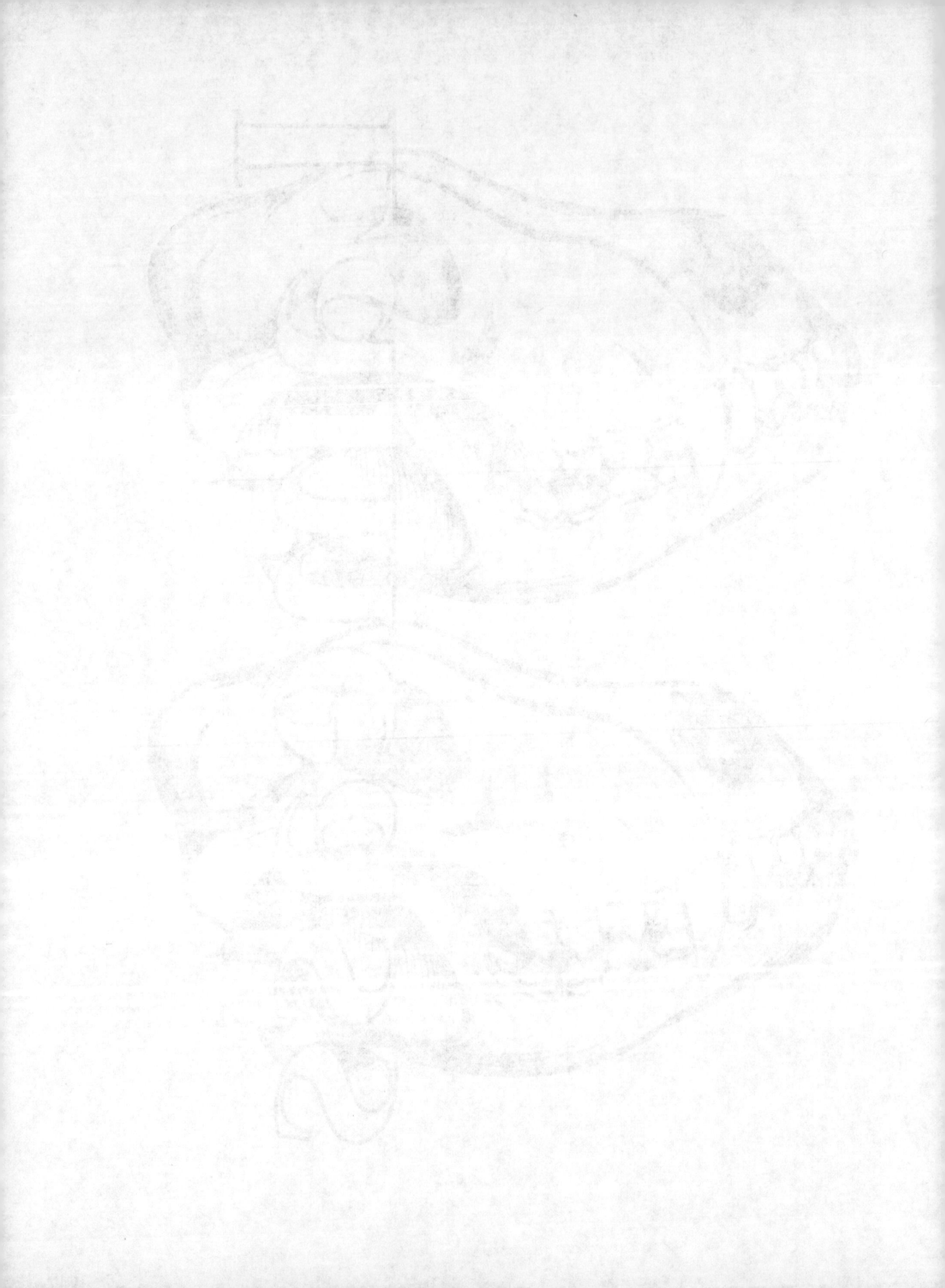

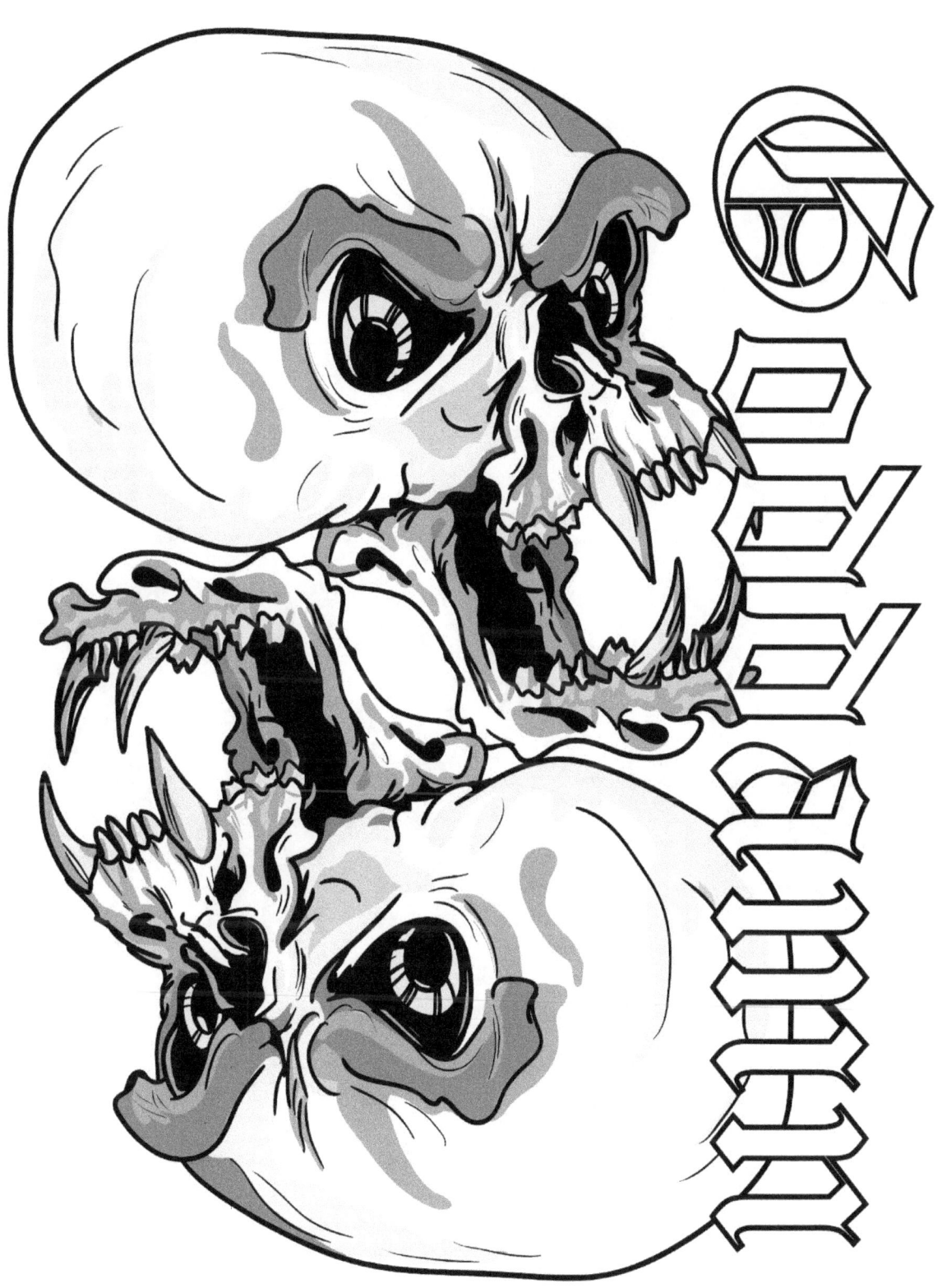

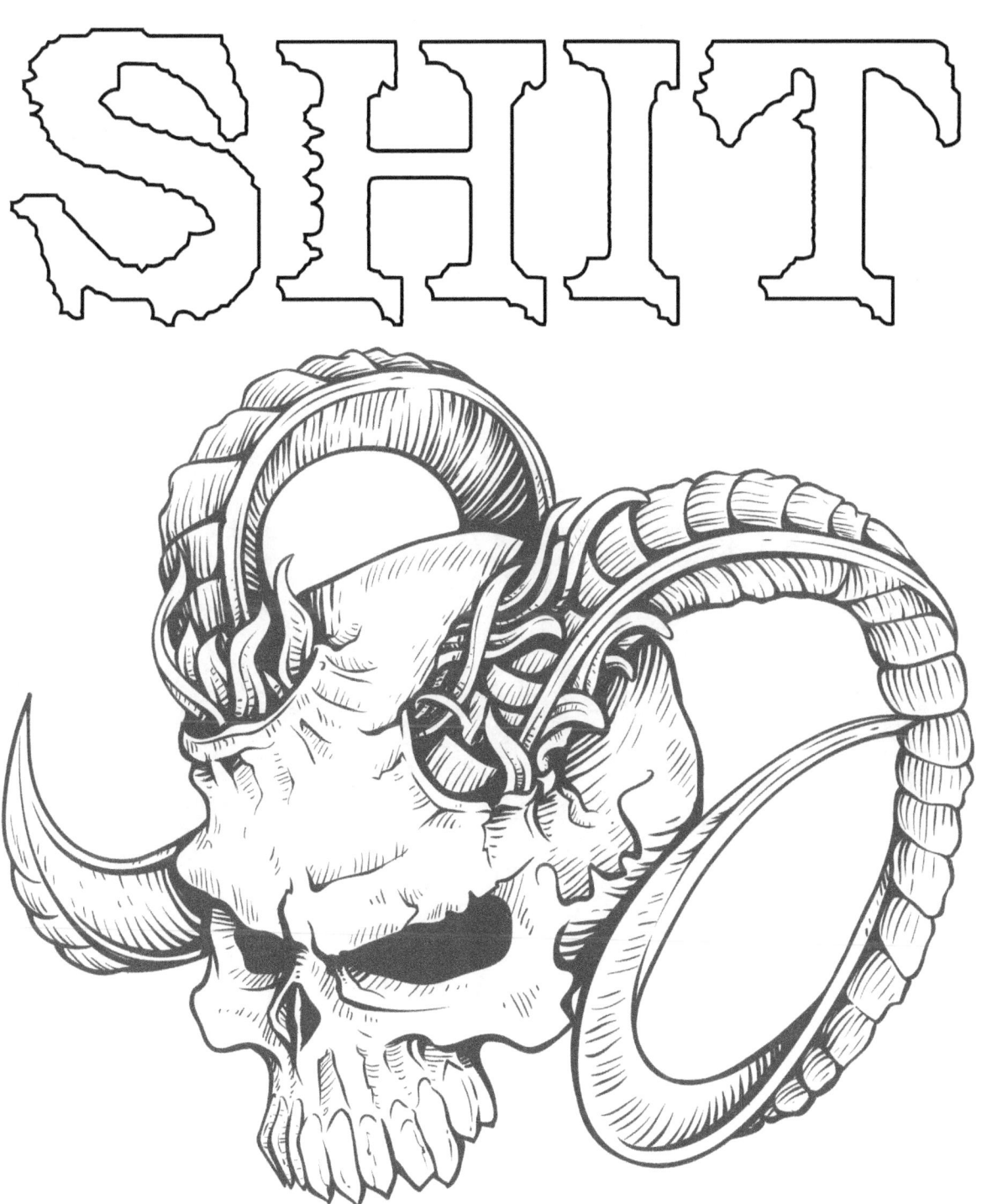

Damn

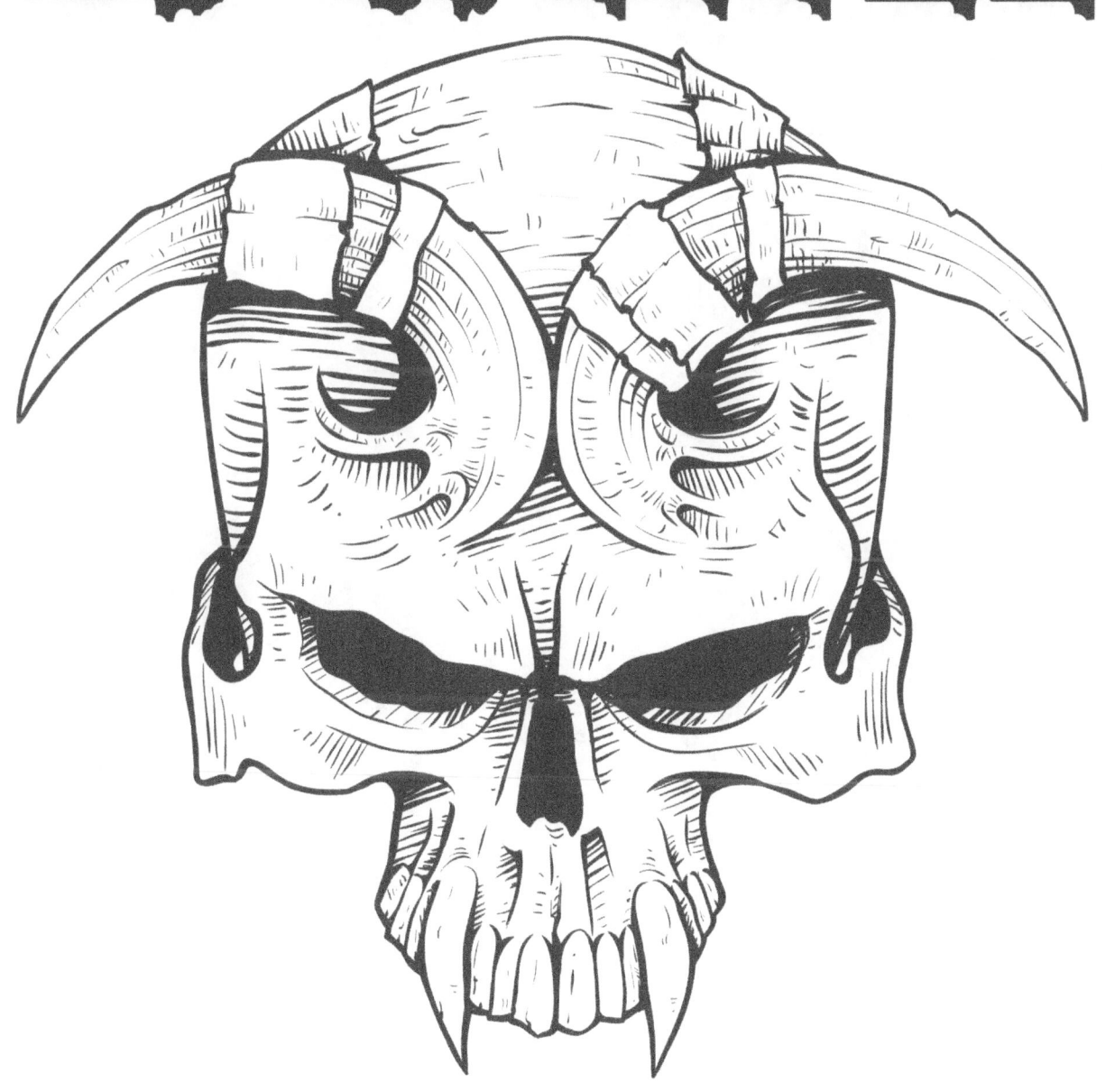

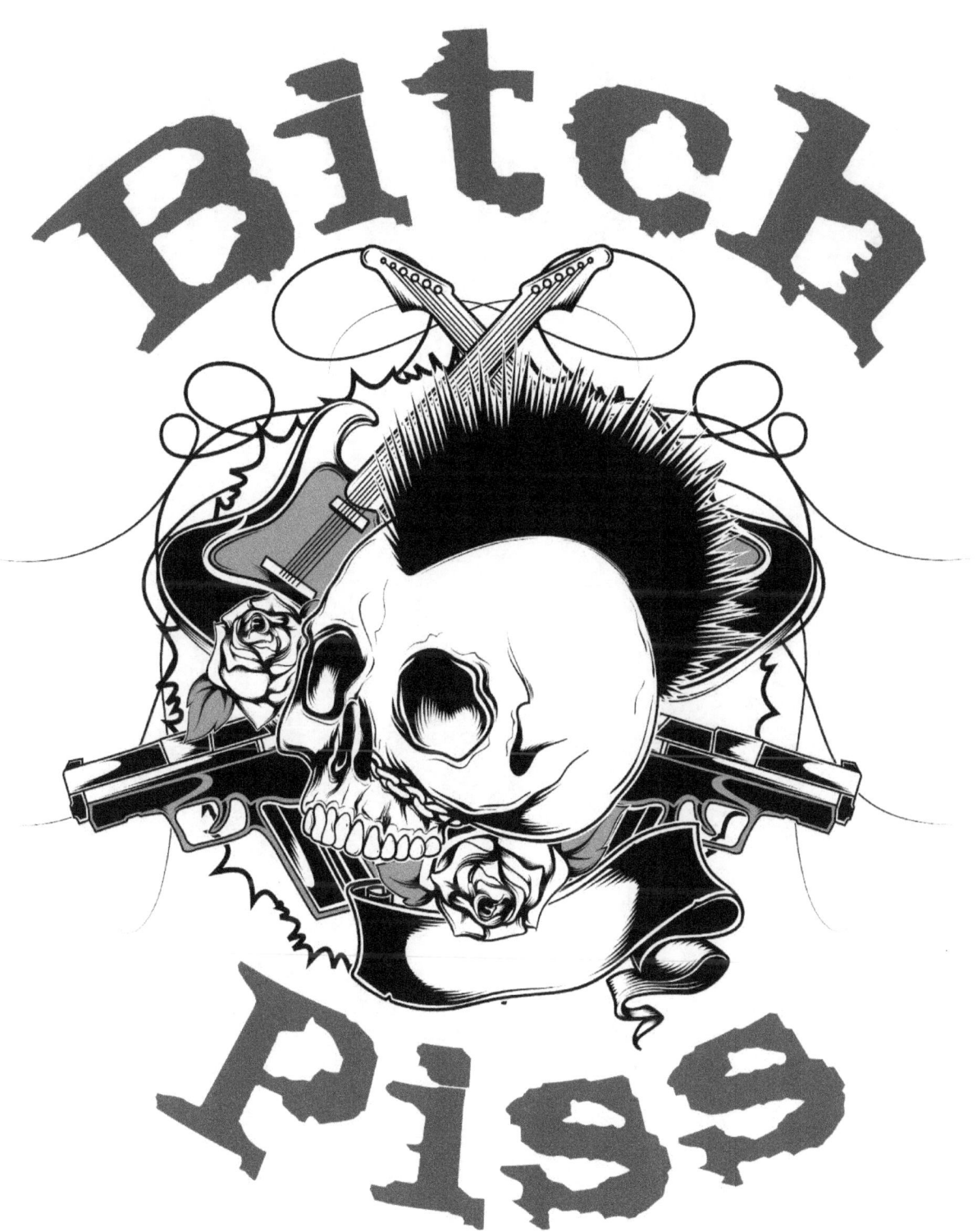

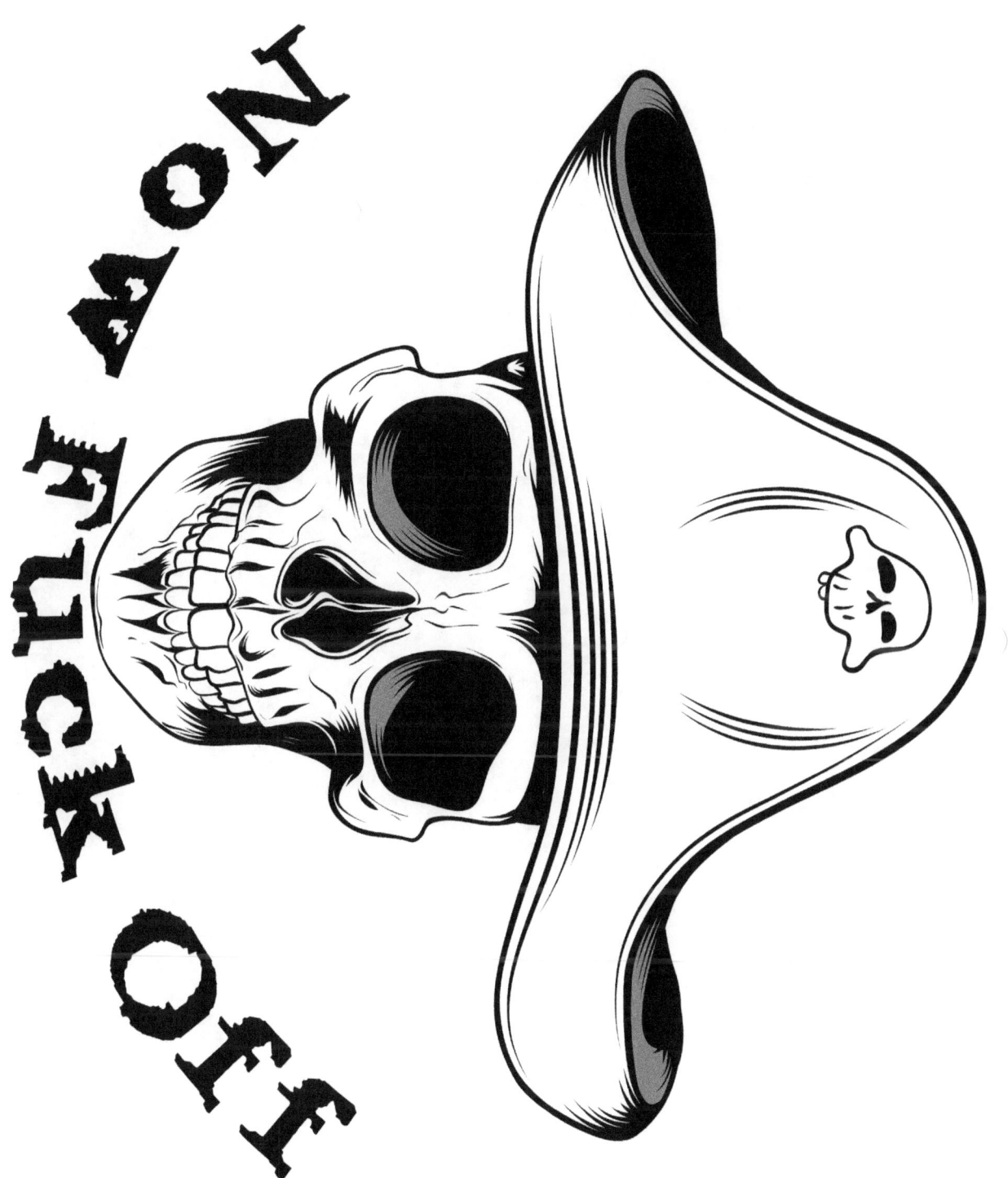

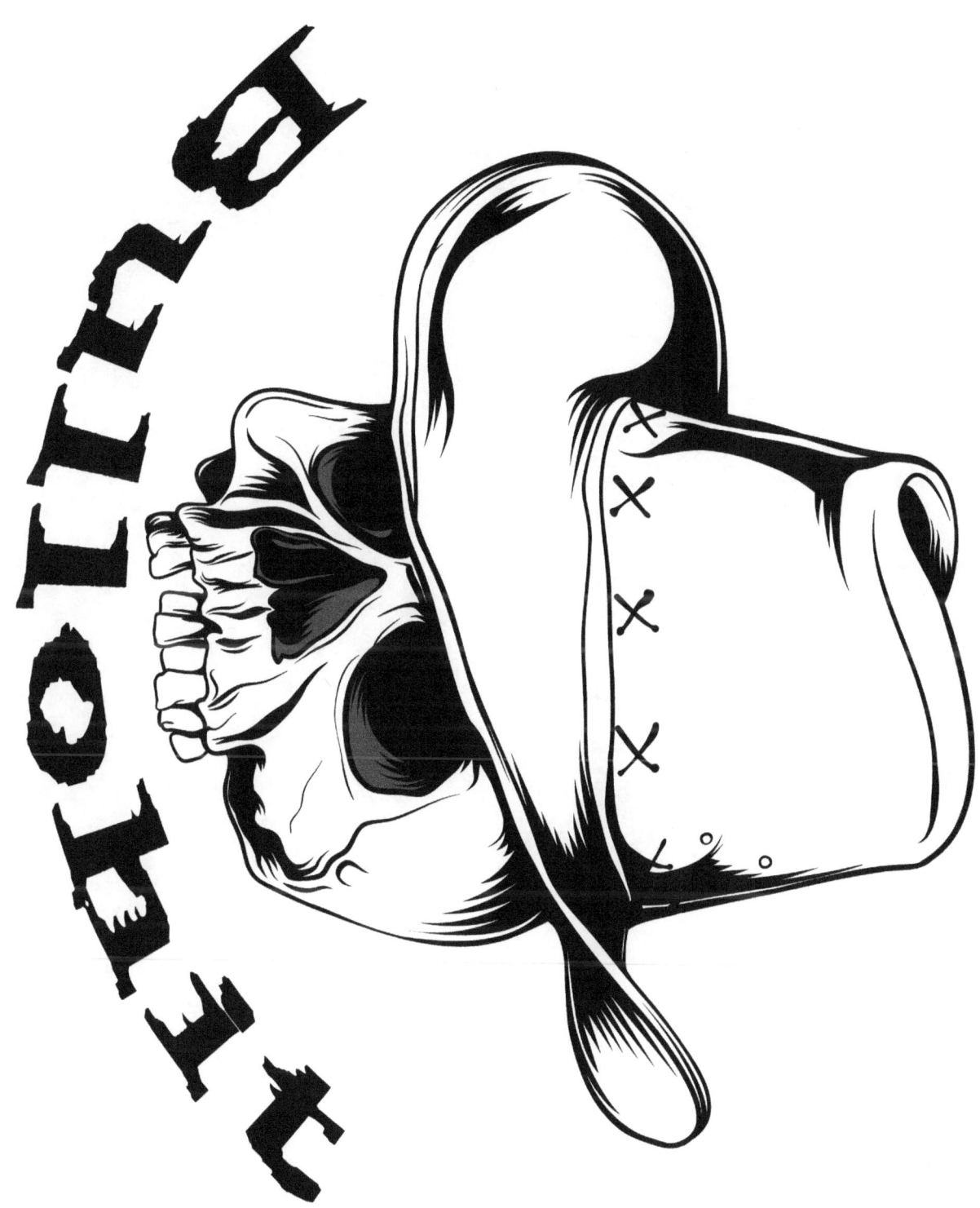

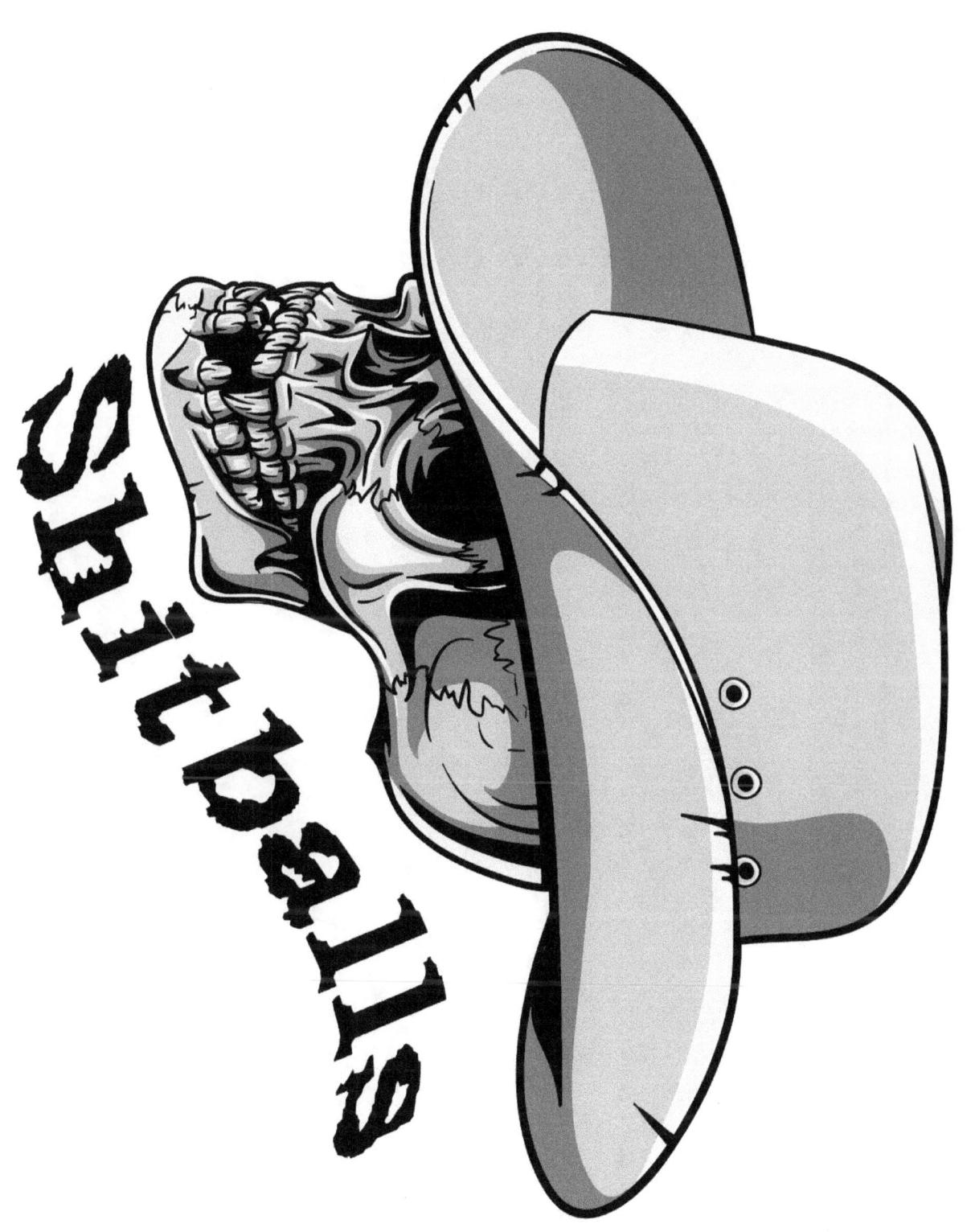

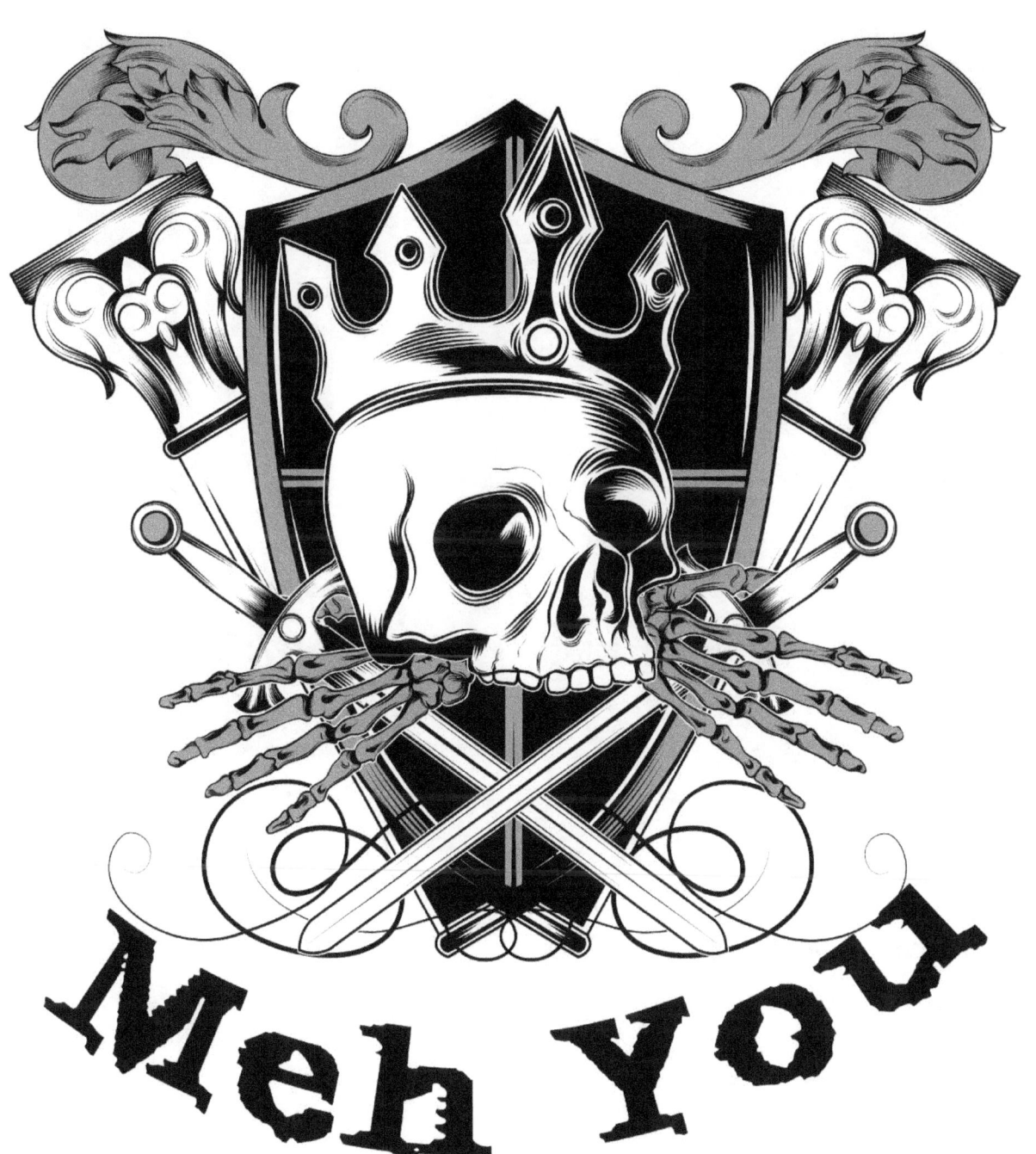

Meh You

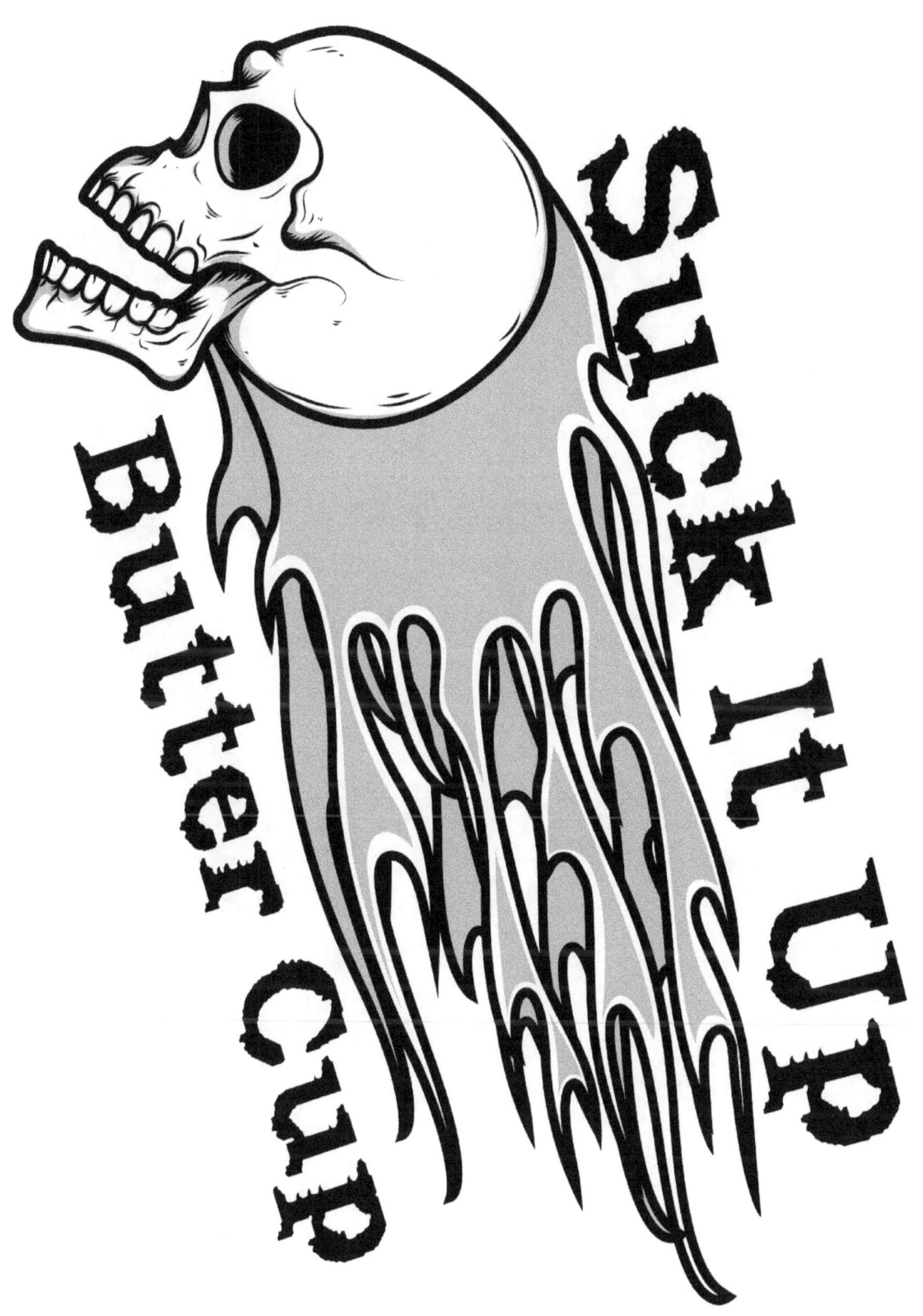

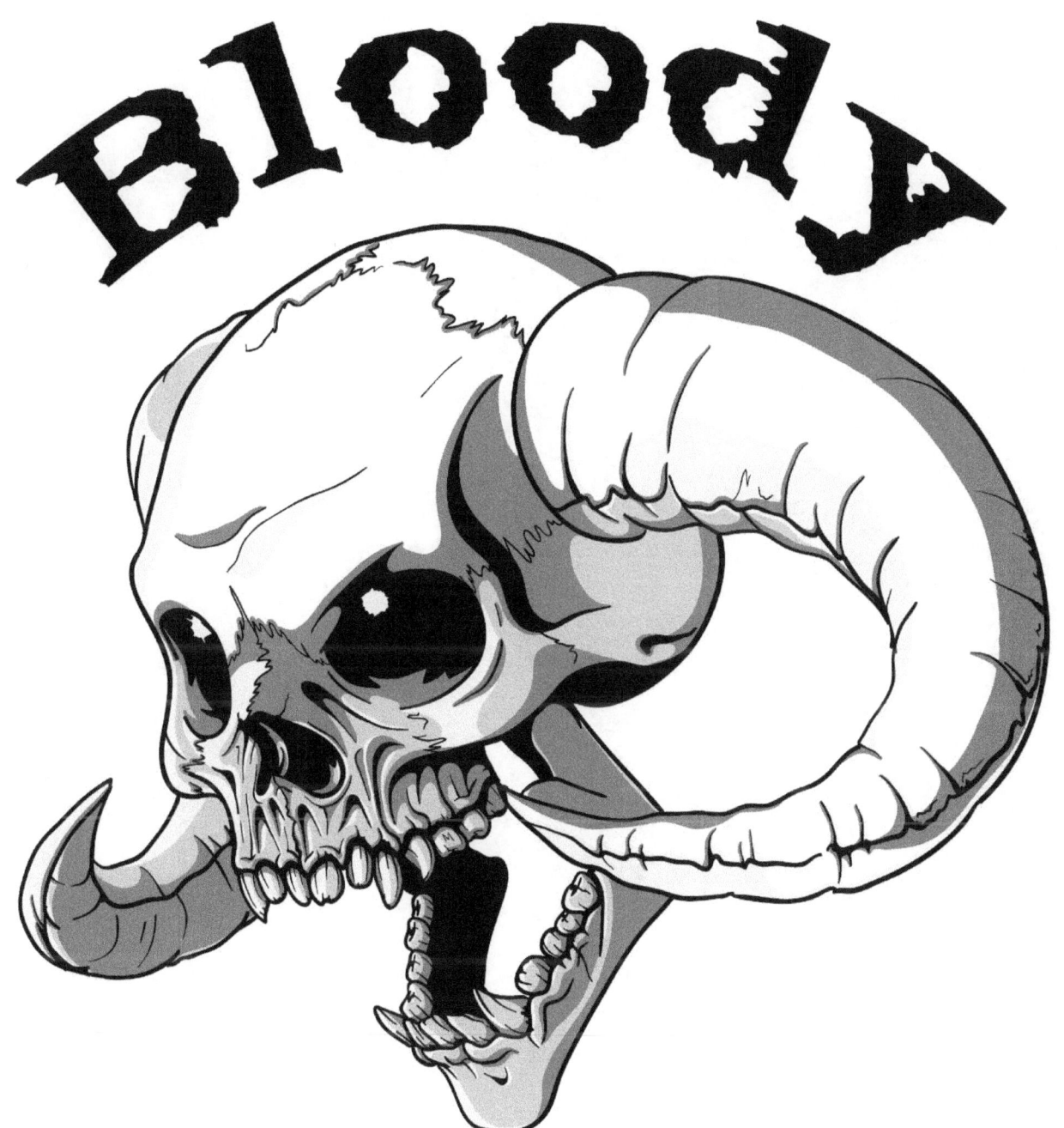

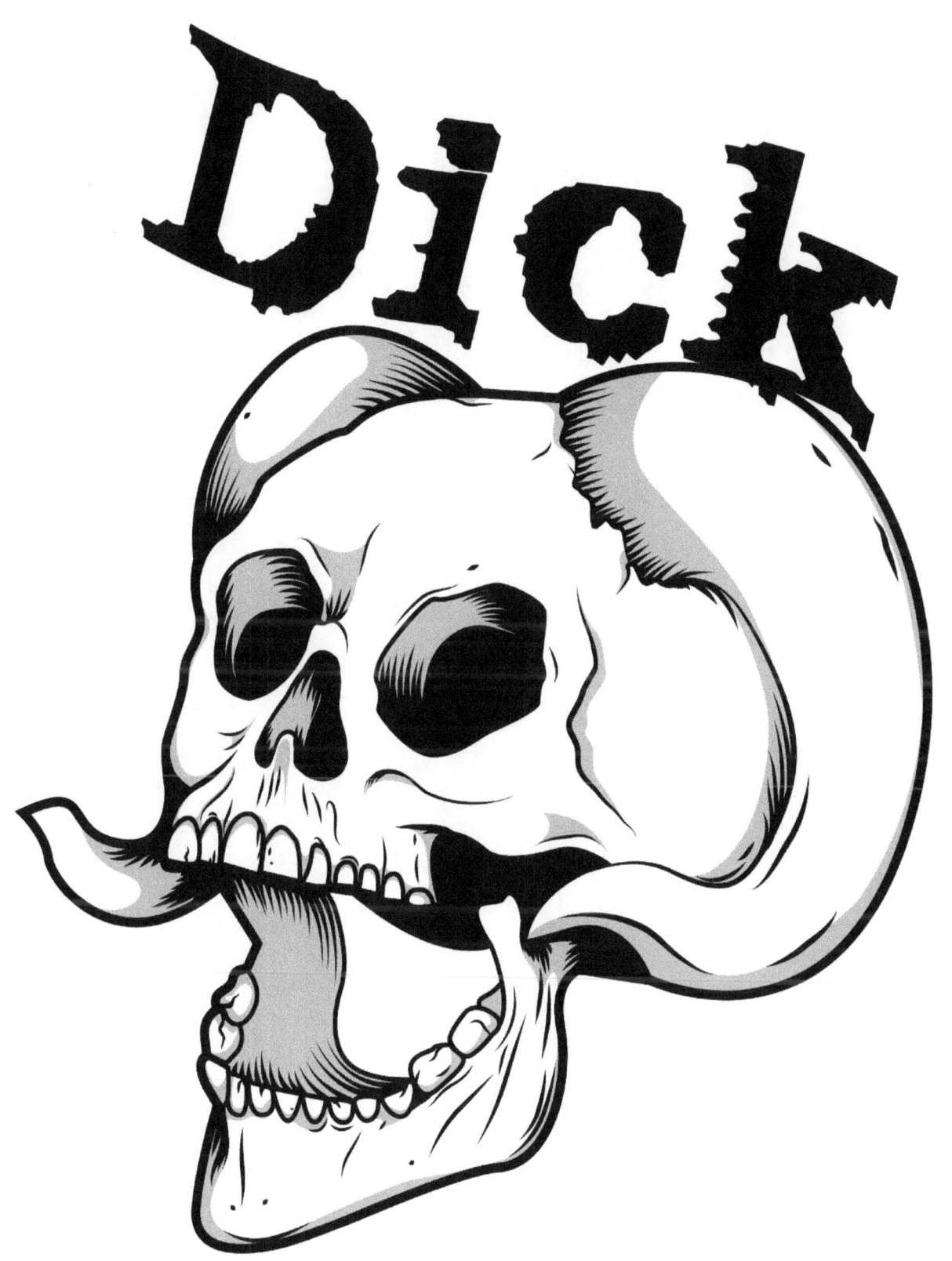

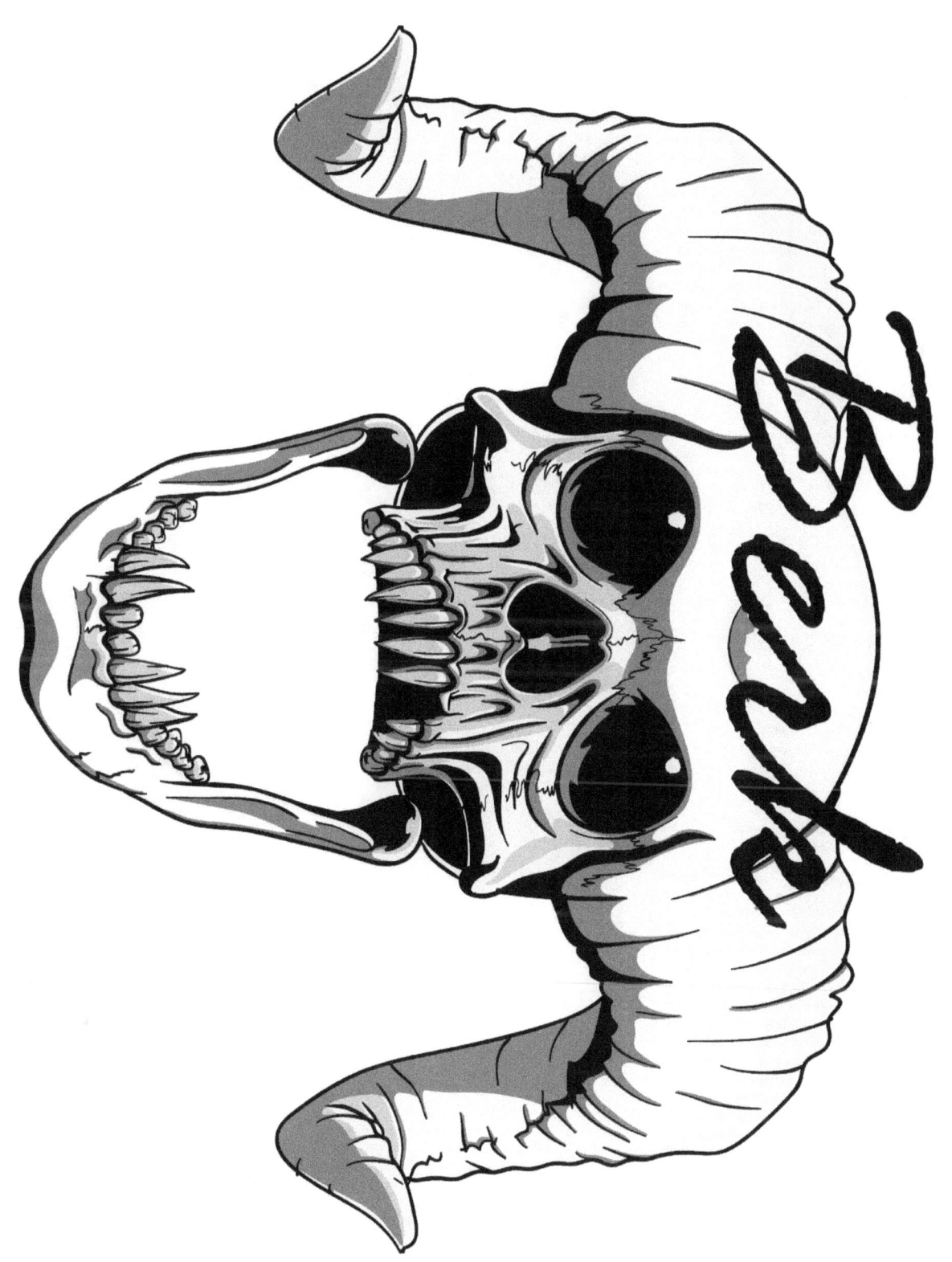

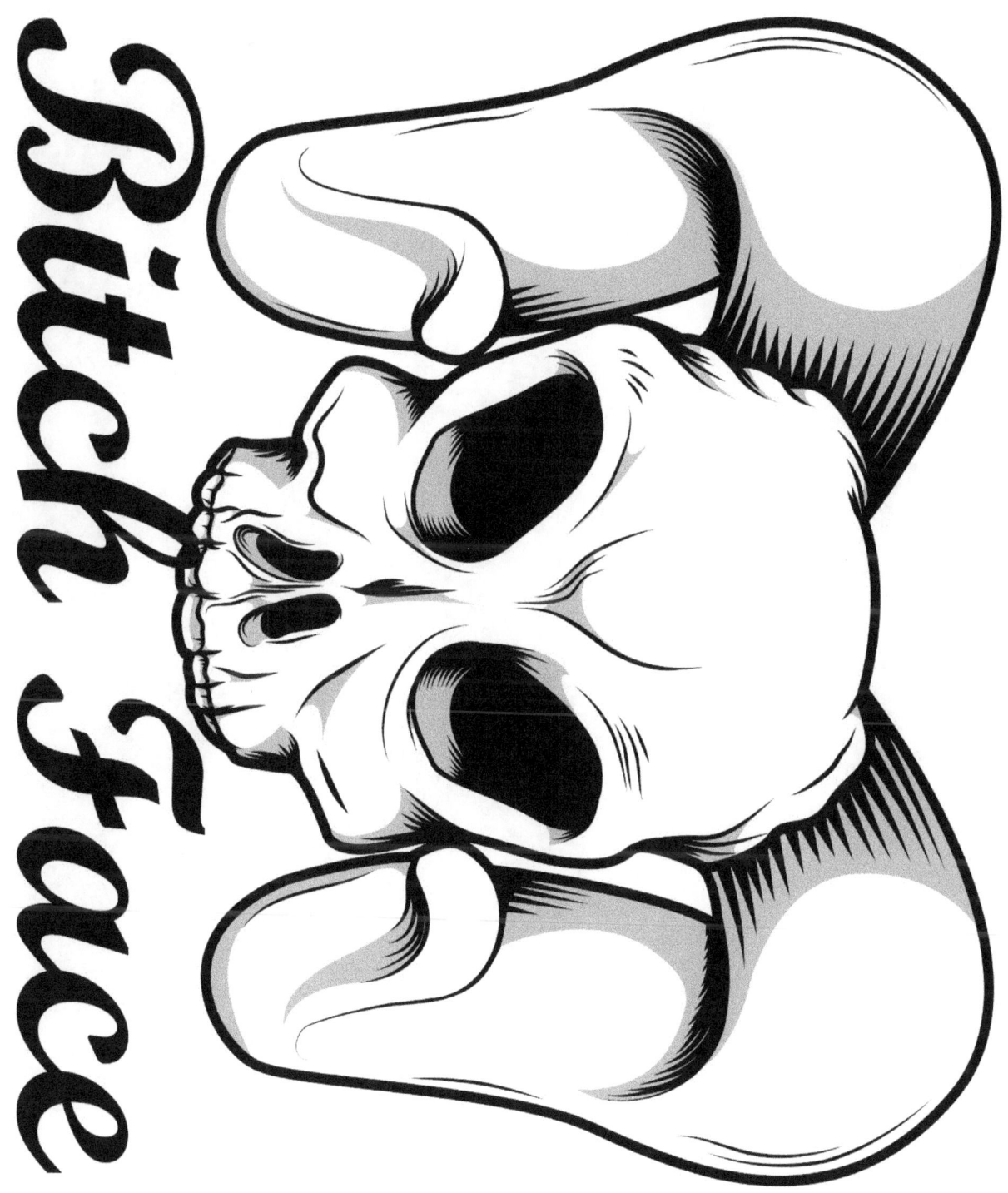

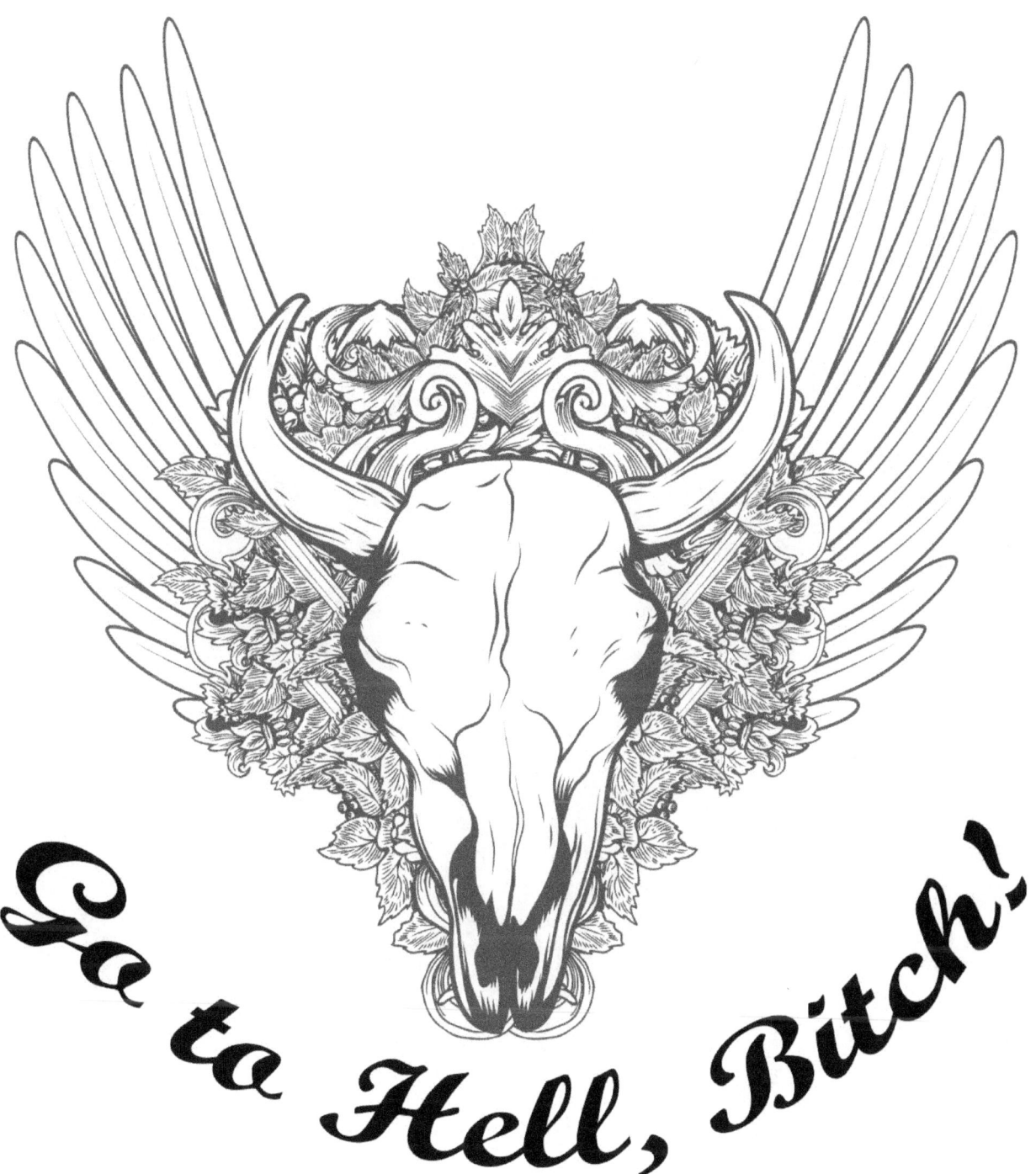

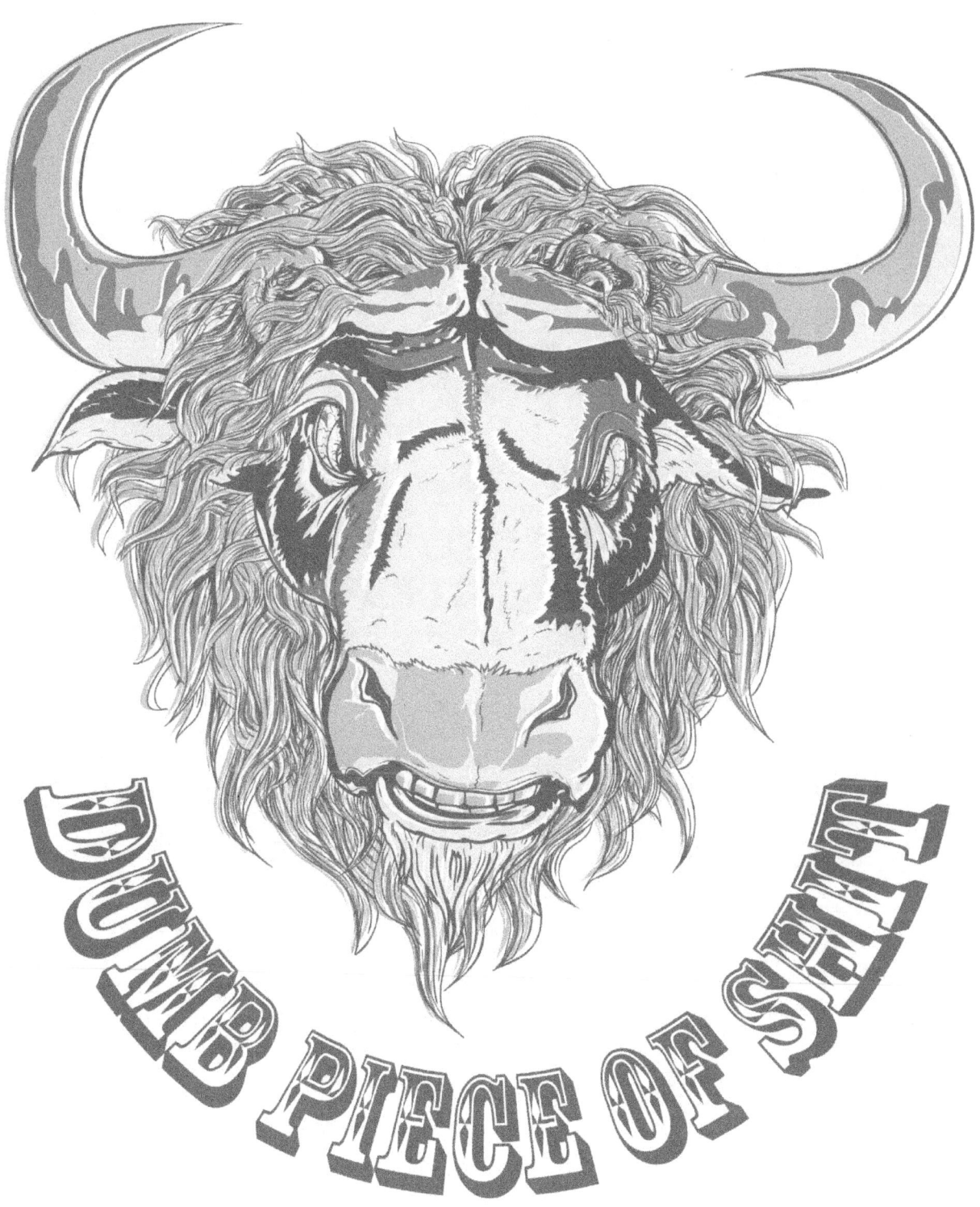

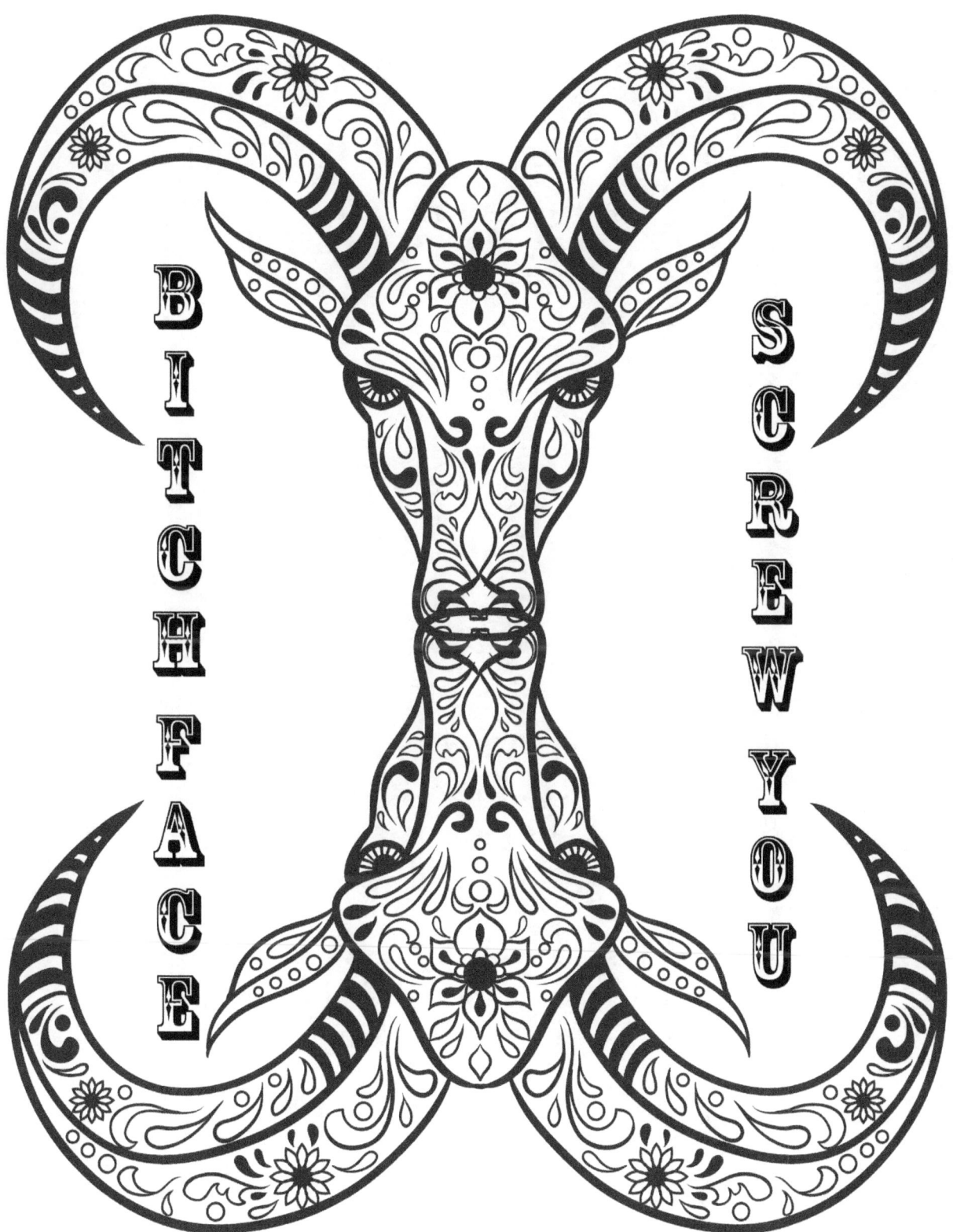

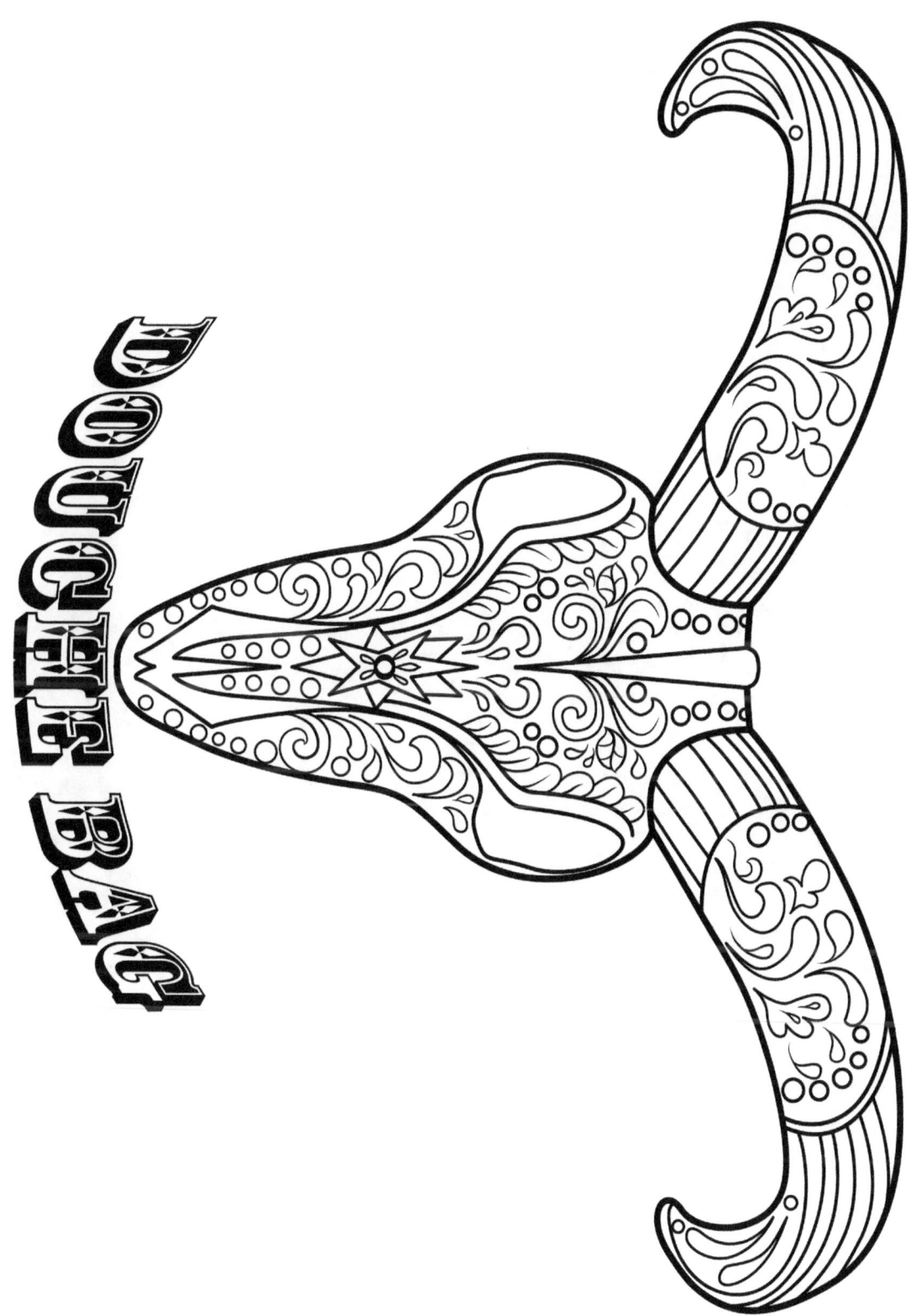

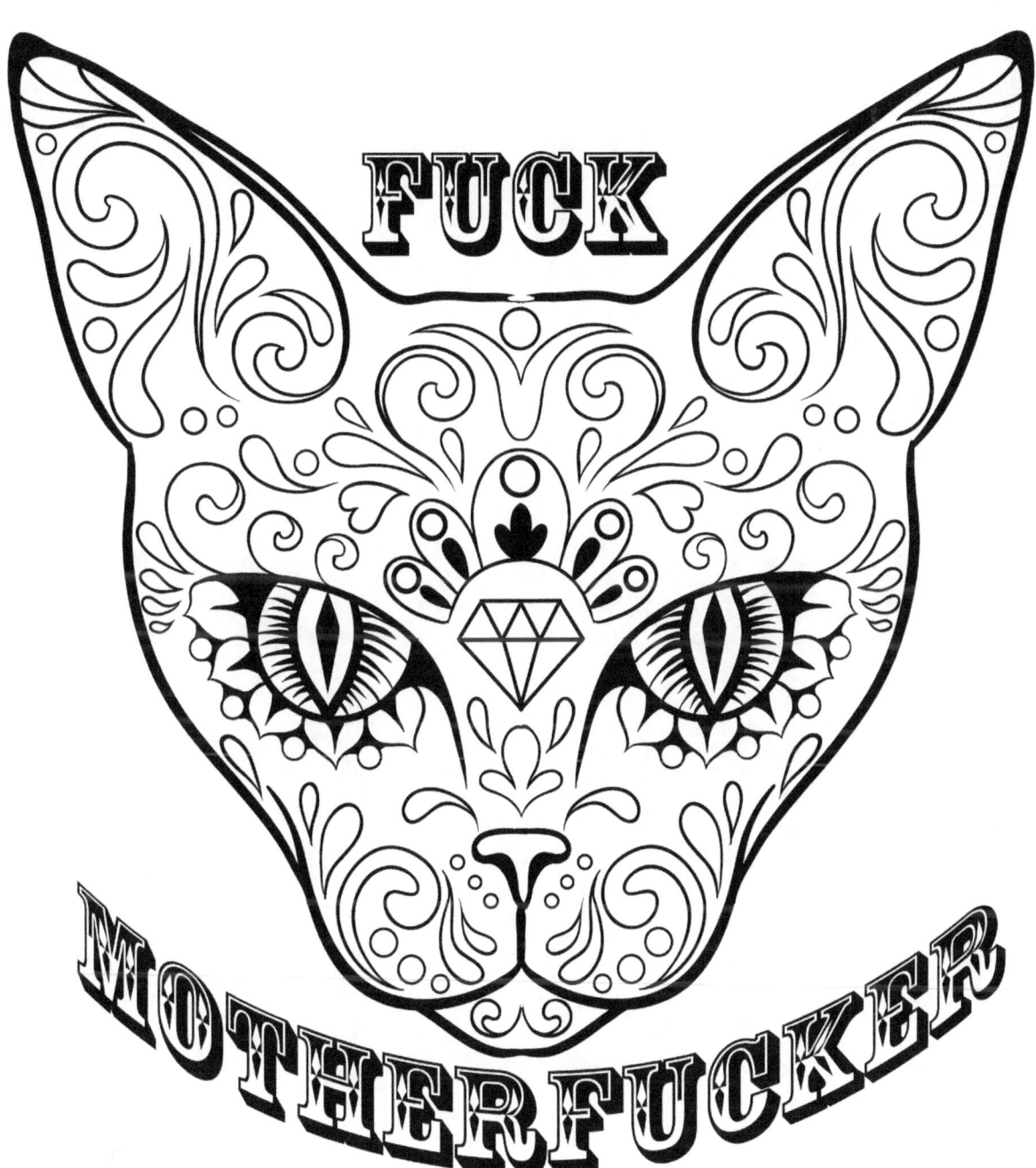

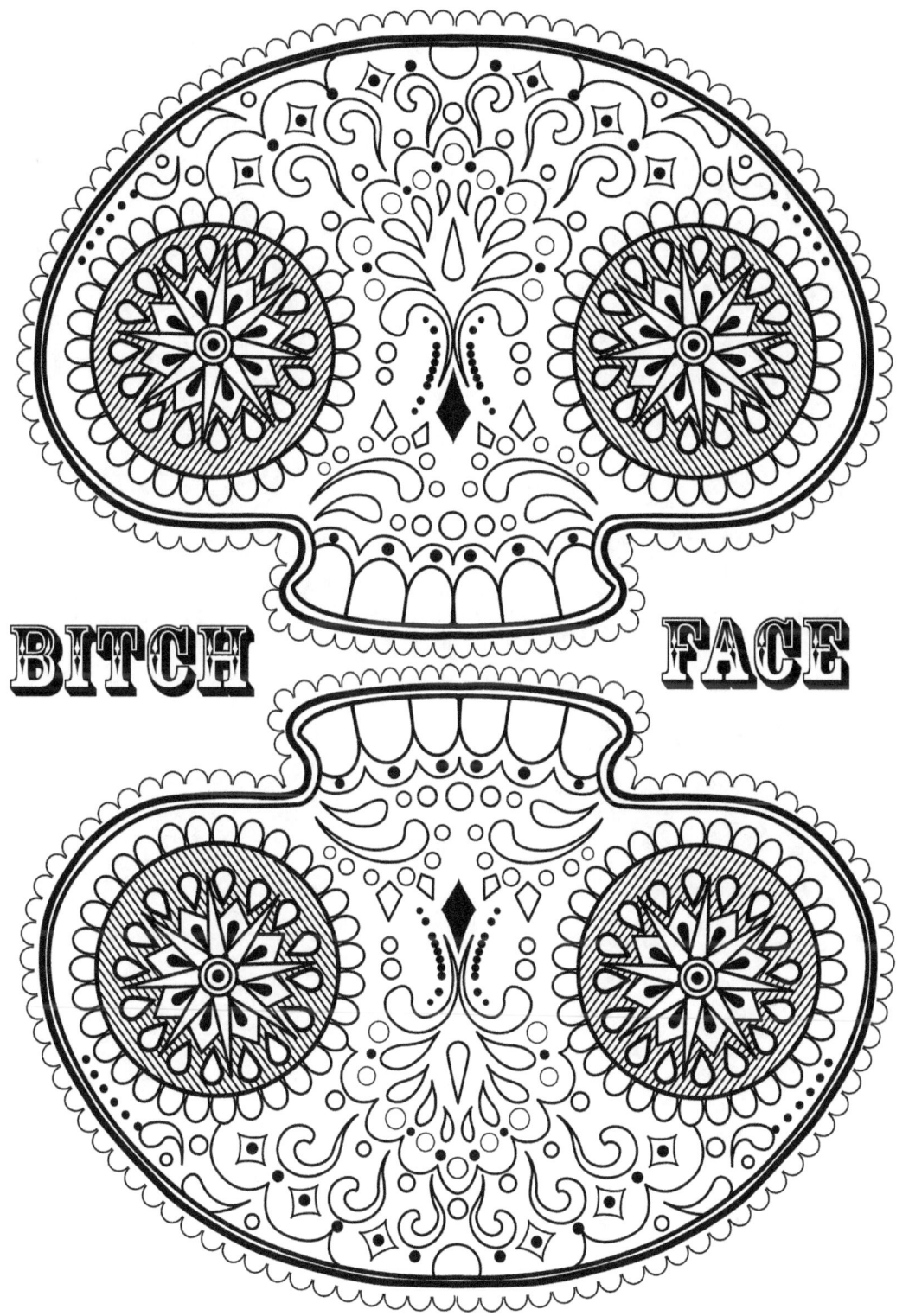

BITCH FACE

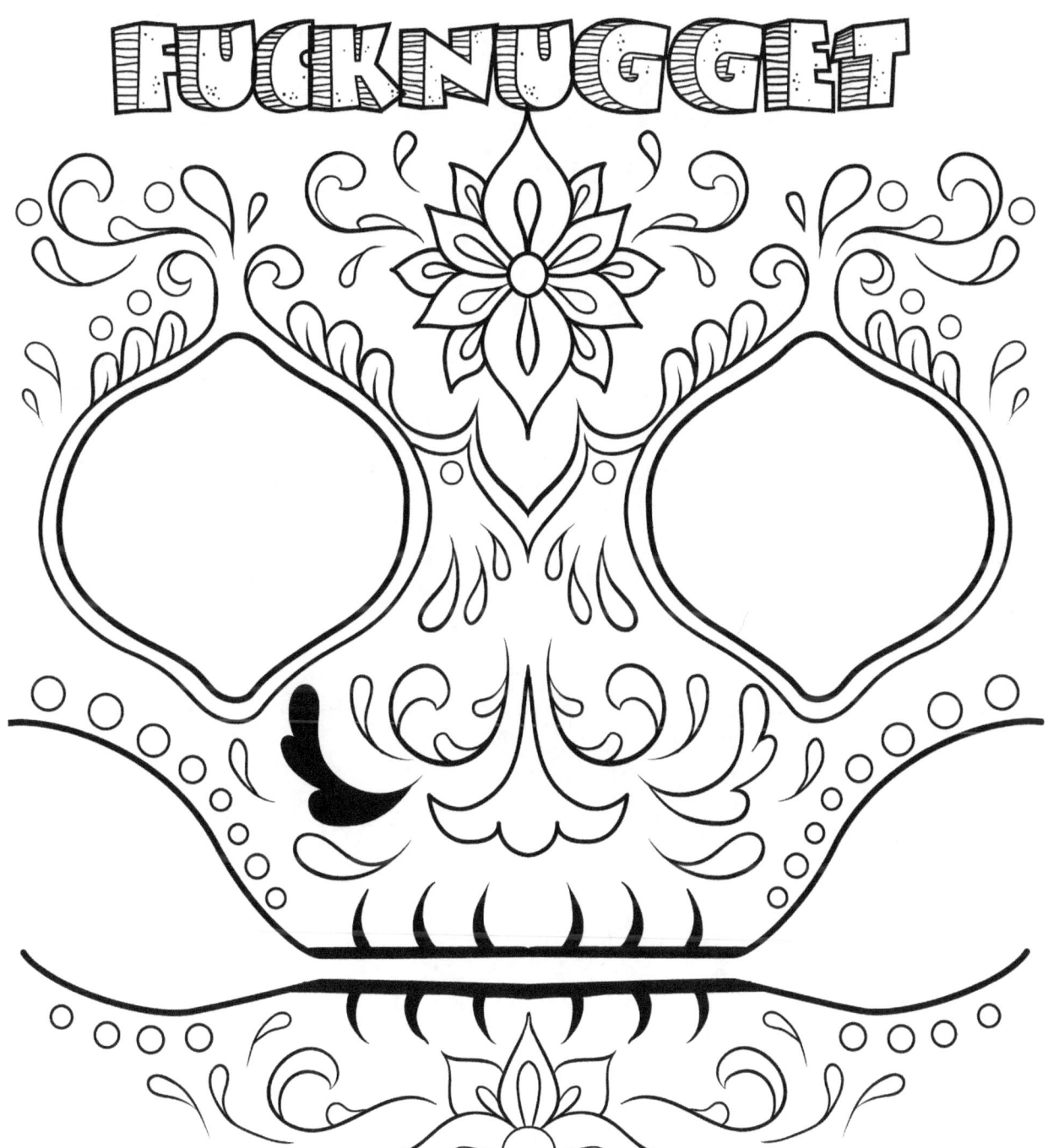

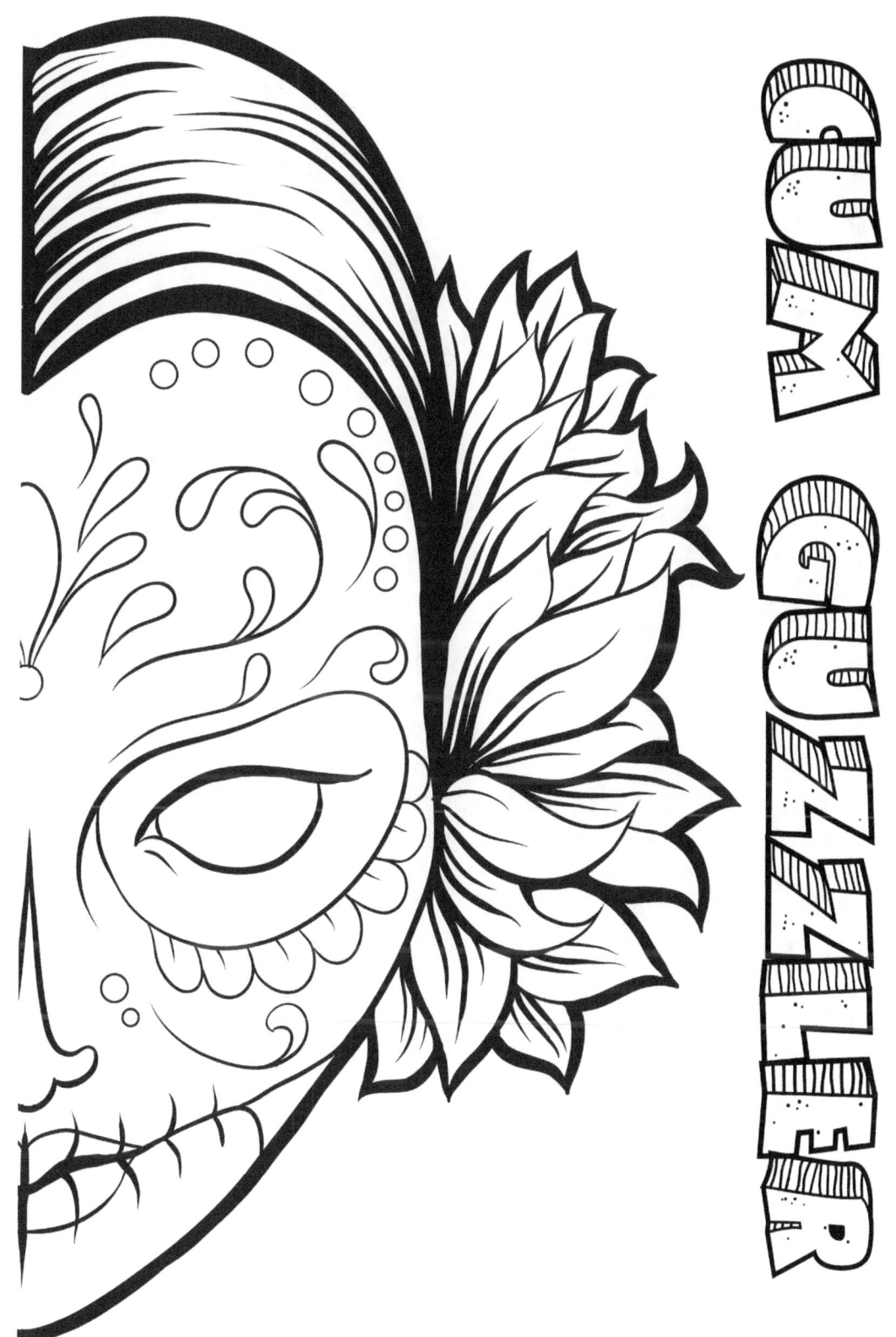

CUM GUZZLER

Thank You

Hope you've enjoyed your reading experience.

We here at Adult Coloring Book J. Kaiwell will always strive to deliver to you the highest quality guides.

So I'd like to thank you for supporting us and reading until the very end.

Before you go, would you mind leaving us a review on Amazon?

It will mean a lot to us and support us creating high quality guides for you in the future.

Thanks once again and here's where you can leave a review.

Warmly yours,
The Adult Coloring Book J. Kaiwell Team

www.ingramcontent.com/pod-product-compliance
Lightning Source LLC
Chambersburg PA
CBHW080628190526
45169CB00009B/3325